How to Kill a Billionaire

How to Kill a Billionaire

BY

Rajesh Talwar

KALPAZ

First Published, 2020

Published by

Kalpaz Publications
C-30, Satyawati Nagar,
Delhi – 110052
Ph.: 011-47034999, 9811692060
www.kalpazpublications.com
E-mail: kalpaz@hotmail.com

Printed at: G. Print Process, Delhi

Cataloging in Publication Data—DK
Courtesy: D.K. Agencies (P) Ltd. <docinfo@dkagencies.com>

Talwar, Rajesh, author.
How to kill a billionaire / by Rajesh Talwar.
pages cm
Novel.
ISBN 9789353242428

1. Indic fiction (English) I. Title.

LCC PR9499.4.T35H69 2020 | DDC 823.92 23

Dedication

For Mom and Dad

Contents

Synopsis 9
Acknowledgments 11

Part One: On An Empty Stomach 13
Part Two 21
Part Three: Breakfast 45
Part Four 69
Part Five: Tea-break 85
Part Six 95
Part Seven: Lunch 127
Part Eight: Cocktails 137
Part Nine: A Last Supper? 153

Synopsis

A billionaire's son goes missing. A young girl commits suicide after a rape. This is a twisted, ironic tale of a brother's love for his sister and his faith in vengeance as the only alternative to a deeply flawed justice system. The brother, a trial court lawyer practising in the lower courts of Delhi, uses the weaknesses of the legal system to confront and confound one of the world's richest men. The story that unfolds takes the reader through the labyrinthine corridors of the Indian legal system to a shattering climax.

Acknowledgments

For their suggestions, support and encouragement I would like to thank Kumkum Jain, Simon Peter Thomas, Tejinder Ahuja, Laxmi Kant Gaur, Ravi Avasthi, Dr Sahni, Praveen Talwar, Narendra S, Narendra Laljani, Simon Peter Thomas, Ayesha Karim, Mansour Jafarian, Mai Trung, Sagari Chhabra, Surya Sinha, Sakshi Talwar, Sanjiv, Sumit, Dhruv, Geet, Puneet, Abhishek, Abhinav, Simi, Alka, , Koshan Jelani, Joanna Paul, Yoon, Tum Zinta, Anita Misra, Kareesha and Zubair Ahmed. A special word of thanks to Amish Raj Mulmi and Linden Stafford for a marvellous edit.

Part One
On An Empty Stomach

1

Good morning, Lord Patel. I hope I haven't kept you waiting for too long, Lord Patel. Or, if I were to call you by your full name, Daulat Ram Laxmi Patel. Why did your parents give you such a long name? In those days it was the practice, I guess, but perhaps also because they had high hopes of you. Daulat means wealth in Hindi, Ram is one of the most important Indian gods, and Laxmi of course is the goddess of wealth. So they were invoking the blessings of two powerful gods – and indeed they were right, for an unending tsunami of money has kept flooding in ever since you started your business. I wonder if anything would have changed had my parents given me a different name.

Too many Patels in the world, your parents might have thought to themselves – not only in India, but also in Leicester, where you were born – and perhaps that's why they decided to give you a more distinctive name. D.R.L. Patel, shorter than V.K.R.V. Rao, that great Indian scholar, but still impressive.

They didn't foresee, in what with hindsight we can call their naïvety, that those initials would be a far inferior title to the ones you would eventually hold. You've received honorary doctorates from Oxford and from Harvard, your alma mater. Five years ago you were knighted by the Queen of England for services to the community. So you became Sir Laxmi Patel. Then last year you were awarded a life peerage for services to business. And so you are now Lord Patel.

You contribute a million pounds every election year to the Conservative Party as well as to Labour. A few hundred thousand to the Lib Dems as well for good measure. It's worth spending this money, for it'll all come back, many times multiplied. As a good businessman you realise that, of course.

I see from your expression that you are surprised. No, surprised is not the word perhaps. Astonished, more like it. You didn't expect this level of English or quality of expression from a lawyer practising in these courts, did you? Well, this will be the first of many surprises for you today, Lord

Patel, I can tell you that. You did not get the full measure of me the last time we met, I believe.

For the past few months, Lord Patel, you've been trying to find out what happened to your son, haven't you? Amit Patel was last seen in the lobby of the Hyatt Regency hotel at six in the evening, and then he suddenly disappeared. Into thin air. He hasn't been heard of since. Your hopes of finding out what had happened to him were raised when the Sessions Judge agreed to hear your complaint against me, in which you accused me of having kidnapped your son. That was, to put it mildly, the very least of your accusations against me, for possibly – or so averred the petition prepared by your lawyers Singhania and Kapoor, and no doubt approved by you – after the kidnapping I might have tortured your son, or even murdered him, as I had threatened to do.

Anyhow, you were packing your bags to go back to England, where your wife – your second, English wife, not your son's mother – waited for you in your luxurious house in South Kensington. Am I right? From your slight nod, I surmise that I must have guessed your travel plans accurately. And then last week, out of the blue, you get an SMS on your private mobile asking you to check your mailbox for a white envelope that would have been delivered only the previous day if you wanted to discover what had happened to your son. You tried to call the number from which the text had been sent, but there was no response. Then you immediately summoned your personal assistant, and asked him to bring to you all the white envelopes that had arrived the previous day. Yes, even in this day and age of internet technology, someone of your eminence gets a fair amount of regular mail. Most of it consists of invitations to parties and gatherings, I'm sure, and even the white envelope that you had been asked to search for contained an invitation. An unusual and unexpected one, for it was an invitation from me asking you to visit me in my chambers today. Unaccompanied, and without informing the police. So you delayed your return to the UK and decided to come and see me.

Inside the white envelope was an unsigned letter, on plain white paper, asking you to visit my office on Sunday – that's today – at nine in the morning. Your name and address were typed on the envelope and the letter inside bore a typed invitation, with my name and address underneath, also typed. In other words, there was no handwriting specimen or even a signature below the invitation. Still, it had been brought to you by your assistant, and you might have opened the envelope in his presence, and it might therefore have crossed your mind that you could rush to the court and adduce it as an additional piece of evidence implicating me in the disappearance of your son. I'm sure the thought entered your mind, but you dismissed the idea after a few moments of reflection, for a successful man like you is unlikely to make the same mistake twice: to have faith in the administration of justice in this country.

You have come to me with high expectations, Lord Patel, and I will not disappoint you. Today you will discover what happened to your son, and I will tell you where he is before the day is over.

I hope you're not in a hurry. No? I'm glad, because while I will tell you all that I know about your son, and what happened to him, it may take a bit of telling, and we will come to it by and by.

Would you like a glass of water? No, you are fine.

Did you leave your car in the car park and walk across to my chambers? No problem in finding the place? I'm glad. Yes, I know it's a ten-minute walk, but I'm afraid that's the only way. Some years ago they did allow cars to drive right up to the chambers, but then it all became such a mess because the lanes between the chambers are so narrow.

It's laughable, you know, the way these lawyers' chambers have been laid out. They are mostly small eight-by-ten-feet plots of land, on which the lawyers to whom they were allotted have had to build their offices, and in between are all these empty spaces and narrow lanes. A much better way to utilise the space would have been to construct a high-rise building and allot offices, just as they've done at the Delhi High Court and with the New Block of Supreme Court Lawyers' Chambers. Anyone with a modicum of common sense, let alone architectural vision, would not have approved the plan, one would have thought, but that's how it is.

The layout of these cramped offices might give a visitor such as you the absurd idea that he's arrived at a section of a large prison – perhaps one of your spacious American correctional institutions – where everyone is in solitary confinement. And yet, when you stop to think of it, perhaps this is a prison, for the lawyers as well as their clients. For lawyers, once they get used to this life, it's very difficult to adjust to any other vocation. For the clients, once they enter the hallowed portals of any of the hundred-odd trial courts located in the adjacent court building – whether as plaintiff or defendant – the chances are that they will spend half a lifetime there before their case reaches any resolution or receives judgement.

A prison is what the Thirty Thousand Courts complex might seem like to an outsider, but there are other ways of viewing the layout. As I mentioned earlier, there are these small chambers, offices mostly eight-by-ten, and then there is a gap of some ten feet, after which there is another office, and this ten-foot gap is uniform in all directions. I sometimes imagine that if I was in an aircraft flying close to the Thirty Thousand Courts I would see the lawyers' chambers all laid out like the squares on a gigantic chessboard, with the chambers representing the black squares and the gaps between them the white squares – it doesn't really matter either way. You could argue that the judicial system is very much like a chessboard too, with the prosecutor making one move and then the defence reacting with a counter-move. Let me assure you, however, that this is simply a rudimentary, little-thought-about and poor design – carved out somewhat in the manner in which colonial powers, such as the British, carved out their erstwhile territories when they were leaving the natives in charge.

I was lucky enough to be allotted a corner plot at the very end of a row. This gives me privacy, and it is actually very quiet here, especially in the evenings. I can see the street from my window, and some evenings when it is late and the light is fading, I take a chair outside to read, or perhaps to study a petition. I can read quite clearly there, for the streetlight on the road adjoining the chambers shines bright.

You want to know if I have recently had my chambers done up. Well spotted! I had the walls painted and the furniture polished only a few months ago. You observe that there are some nails in the wall behind me, and several scratches on the wall, as if some shelves might have been hanging there earlier. As a matter of fact, you are right again, Lord Patel. This is why you have become a billionaire and a lord! What else have you noticed or concluded in the short time you have been in my chamber? Possibly more than a frequent visitor might have noticed in ten visits.

True, there used to be a fine pinewood bookcase hanging on those walls, but then the carpenter told me that the contractor who had constructed my chambers had cheated me, and had put too much sand and too little cement in the building material for these walls to bear the burden of such big shelves laden with thick, voluminous legal texts. I could have kept the shelves – they were not so heavy by themselves, and most attractive – but it would surely have looked odd to a visitor; they would have been empty, without any law reports, legal commentaries or what have you stacked on them. So I got the shelves dismantled and took them home, where they occupy pride of place in a room that now serves as my office. My sister Ruhno used to sleep in that room when she came to live with me.

You represent a new breed of businessman, Lord Patel – a well-qualified, educated businessman; with globalisation, you need a full knowledge of the world if you want to do big business. You made sure that your son Amit attended one of the best business schools in the world. What was it called? The Wharton Business School of Management. One of the best, but perhaps not the very best.

On the other hand, you yourself, Lord Patel, although British-born, went to pursue your studies in a law school in the United States. I can see your expression of pleased surprise. You are too modest. Don't you know that your background has been mentioned in hundreds of newspapers? And I for one have certainly been interested in your life experience. As I recall from my reading of your bio, your initial plan – and that of your parents for you – was to become a lawyer, someone like myself, though of course a lawyer practising on a much more elevated platform, so your parents sent you to the best-known law school in the world, the Harvard Law School – which is where, incidentally, the current President of the United States also studied.

You studied law at Harvard, and you learned how legal systems operate the world over: the common law system, the civil law system, Islamic legal systems and various hybrids. But my feeling is that you didn't learn how legal systems outside the developed world operate in reality.

You will forgive me if I try to make up this deficiency in your background by occasionally rambling on about how the business of the lower courts works in this country. I will try to give you a crash course in their functioning. If I may say so, I don't think the reverse would be possible. I mean, I don't think it would be possible for you to give me a crash course in what you learned at Harvard. You smile. Do I detect some condescension there?

You've come to meet me only because you think I may have some idea where your son might be. Isn't that true? The great Lord Patel, coming to the Thirty Thousand Courts, to see a lowly, underpaid lawyer like myself, sitting in his small smelly cabin waiting for him to appear.

Everyone waits for you normally, don't they? Even kings and prime ministers, or so I hear. You're used to being waited upon. And yet you were careful to be on time, and would not have left even if I had been further delayed. Well, I was delayed for a reason, but I will explain that later.

Have you eaten breakfast, by the way? No? You've come to see me on an empty stomach. I haven't eaten either. Quite often I used to have breakfast in my chambers in the mornings, which generally meant a cup of tea, a *fain*, a *mathi* and a couple of Marie biscuits, but I have not resumed the habit. You see, I gave up eating breakfast here when my sister Ruhno came back to live with me a year ago, and now I desist from having breakfast here because it brings back painful memories. The lump in my throat makes it difficult for me to swallow the tea or eat any *fain*. But today, for your sake, I will join you for a small breakfast.

Part Two

2

One morning, nearly three months after Amit Patel disappeared – an event reported in all the major newspapers – my front doorbell rang.

I wondered if it was the police. It was only a quarter to five and still dark outside – too early for the milkman or the newspaper vendor to bother me, but the right time for law enforcement agencies to make an arrest. Besides, I had been expecting something to happen. I knew enough about Lord Patel, Amit's father, to guess that he would not sit idly by. And I had issued threats I would drag Amit out of his house on Holi, outside Amit's residence, the 'White House', in Golf Links.

In fact, it was that evening he disappeared and was not heard of again.

'*Aap*, sir?' A familiar face from the courts gaped at me as I opened the door.

'Your name is . . .?' I struggled.

'Gopal Ram, sir. I forgot yours too, sir.'

Gopal Ram was one of a hundred process servers at the court, and I was one of three thousand lawyers, so it wasn't surprising that neither of us remembered the other's name.

Despite so many lawyers, Gopal recognised me instantly, and I suspect it had to do with my appearance, which is distinctive, even if it is not memorable.

At six feet nothing, I'm tall by Indian standards, and tower over most of my legal brethren. If you wanted to pay me a compliment you would say that I had chiselled features; if you wished to put me down, you'd say I had a bony face. With the exception of my nose perhaps, I have very little flesh on my face; even my cheeks are a bit sunken, which I'm told gives me a somewhat melancholic look. Women are fond of biting my nose; even Uma, my first girlfriend at university, liked doing that. I'm not sure why, because it doesn't look particularly appetising or large like a pakora; it's rather well proportioned. Perhaps that is why there are some among the female species who – ever so gently – like to sink their teeth into it.

'So what do you have for me, Gopal Ram-ji?' I threw in the respectful *ji*, trying to put him at ease.

'Summons, *saab*.' He looked contrite, almost embarrassed.

Attached to the summons was a complaint typed out on expensive court stationery, the kind used by big law firms. I ran through it rapidly.

The petition averred that I was responsible, either directly or indirectly, for the kidnapping of Amit Patel, owner of Patel Holdings and Properties. It went on to speculate that I either still held Amit in my custody or had murdered him, and that the complainant reserved his right to press additional charges.

I was interested to know what motives had been attributed to me for wanting to kidnap and subsequently murder Amit Patel. It was more or less along the lines that I would have expected.

My sister Ruhno, the petition stated, used to be an employee of Patel Holdings and had during the course of her employment become infatuated with the young and successful Amit Patel. I myself had met with Amit Patel's father in an attempt to fix her marriage with the lord's son. Ever since my sister's accidental death (a photocopy of the hospital records were attached to the complaint), I had begun to imagine that it might not have been an accident but a suicide. And for this suicide I held Amit Patel responsible together with Amit's friend and financial adviser, Sunil Gupta.

Sunil Gupta himself, the petition went on to explain, had been brutally stabbed to death and his body thrown into the Yamuna. The petition did not allege that I had any hand in Sunil Gupta's death, I was amused to note, but threw a strong hint in that direction. Singhania and Kapoor were experienced lawyers and did not want to go off track. Besides, the criminal complaint mechanism was to be used in instances where the complainant was directly affected by the crime, which was clearly the case here, for the petition had been filed by the missing man's father. With Sunil Gupta the connection would not have been so clear. Singhania and Kapoor did not wish to overplay their hand. The large, flowery signature of Lord Patel filled half of the last page of the petition.

But why, I mulled, did Lord Patel need to file this complaint at all? Surely a man of his eminence and power could have simply called on the Law Minister and asked him to ask the Commissioner of Police to slam a case against me. That's what I had been expecting these past three months. I stood beside the window that overlooked Shahid Bhagat Singh Park, where I went for walks in the evening, and looked at the growing light beyond the green fields.

'Everything okay?' Gopal Ram said anxiously.

'Yes, everything is fine,' I assured him. 'Just give me a minute.'

I went over to the kitchen to make tea for us both. As the warm liquid boiled, I allowed it to simmer, boiled it again, and then poured out the milky substance into two thick corrugated glasses. Gopal Ram wouldn't enjoy his tea in fine china, and I would bear him company not only with the tea but with the vessel in which it was contained.

Usually, getting the police to charge me with the criminal offence of murder would have been simple enough for someone like Lord Patel, but there was a complication here. The lawyers from the Thirty Thousand Courts were a plucky lot and would stand by a colleague whom they thought to be wrongfully accused. I began to imagine how it must have happened.

My guess was that the Commissioner would not have been 'helpful' even to a man like Patel because he would have recalled the previous episode when I had been picked up, the lawyer's strike that had followed, the reprimand from the Law Minister, the consequent threat to his own job and position – and this time had decided to be more cautious.

The commissioner had sent a senior superintendent of police to my house to interview me a week or so after Amit's disappearance. '*Vakil, saab*,' said the trim, grey-haired man with the starched uniform. 'This won't take long at all. I have just two or three questions. First of all, can you tell me how and where you celebrated Holi?'

'I remember everything clearly,' I said. 'It was a festival, but, since my sister had only recently passed away, I was in no mood to celebrate.'

He nodded in sympathy, waiting for me to continue.

'I spent the day in my chambers in court preparing cases.'

'And the evening?'

'I spent the evening drinking whisky with a couple of friends at the Sixers, one of the bars inside Delhi Sports Club, till late at night.'

I saw the question in his eyes and provided two names.

'My friends could testify to my presence,' I said, 'but you could also check with the regular bartenders and waiters.'

'One more question, sir. Is it true that you threatened to kidnap Amit Patel on Holi?'

'Kidnap?' I spilled my drink on the table, my eyes smiling, and the amused laughter as natural as I could make it. 'Why would I threaten Amit Patel? Is he nursing a guilty conscience over something?'

'I don't know, sir. As you are aware, he is missing, so I haven't been able to verify this. But this is what one of the security guards at Amit Patel's residence at the White House has claimed.'

One of the security guards at the White House. That must have been the sloppy bastard who insulted me.

'I don't know about any threats,' I said, 'but I remember pulling up one of the security guards for drinking on duty. Must be the same man. Getting a small revenge. You know how people are.'

He noted down everything in a small black book.

'Is there something I should be worried about?' I said, as I saw him to the door.

'No, sir.'

'I mean, I could inform the President of the Bar Association if you have any plans to arrest me.'

'No, no, sir. You embarrass me. This is just a routine inquiry.'

* * *

The man went away, and I never saw him again. So the Commissioner of Police would have told Lord Patel that the police had concluded they didn't have enough grounds for arresting me. If I had issued a threat – this might even be true, he admitted – at the date and time his son disappeared (he was last seen in the lobby of the Hyatt Regency hotel at six in the evening), I was having drinks in the Sixers bar of the Delhi Sports Club. I could imagine Lord Patel and one of his lawyers arguing that there was the additional fact, or bit of circumstantial evidence, that I was the lawyer on record for the case that had resulted in the eviction of Patel's son from his residence, as well as the testimony of the security guard. Still, the Commissioner would have maintained, it wasn't enough. 'File a complaint case against him,' he might have said, 'and if the court directs us we will swing into action. And do everything in our power to help you,' a broad hint at how torture was the shortest cut used by the Indian police in their investigations.

So Lord Patel would've consulted his lawyers, Singhania and Kapoor, and they would've assured him they could fix me through the judicial mechanism of the courts, and having faith in those products of Yale and Harvard, where he himself and his son had trained, he gave them the go-ahead. They would've suggested that a complaint case be filed in the Thirty Thousand Courts, and Patel was willing to try anything that might bring him closer to finding out what had happened to Amit.

And so Singhania and Kapoor had prepared the petition and asked two of their smart young lawyers to file the case and follow up.

All this was pure speculation on my part, but, when you've been in the business for as long as I have, you tend to form a reasonably good estimate of the way these things happen.

'*Aur koi seva*?' Gopal Ram said, as he slurped the tea with evident satisfaction.'

'The judge will adjourn the hearing for another three months, won't he?'

'It could be less,' he said. 'This is a high-profile case.' He put the glass down on the table. 'Maybe two months.'

'Could you talk to the judge's clerk and make it three?'

'Three and a half,' he promised.

'And could you get the summons marked to yourself the next time as well?'

'Not a problem.' He laughed.

'And do a repeat of today's report. What will you write this time?'

'You were not at home. That's it.'

'Okay, and the next time, make it "party out-of-station" instead of "not at home". Okay?'

'All right, sir. Anything else?'

'No,' I said. 'For the time being this should be enough.'

I pulled out my wallet, peeled out two one-thousand-rupee notes, with the face of the incorruptible Gandhi emblazoned across, and pressed these on him.

'This is too much, sir.' He looked startled. 'You know the rate.'

'This is a special case, Gopal Ram. It's important to me.'

'I understand, sir. Believe me, even if the other party offers me a million rupees I won't change my report.'

* * *

Gopal Ram was true to his word. He showed up three and a half months later for a second time.

I gave him another two thousand rupees.

'It'll be the last time for my report, *bauji*,' he said. 'Next time they'll send a constable.'

I nodded. I wanted Lord Patel to wait longer. I wasn't ready just yet.

'But if there is anything else I can do . . .'

'Tomorrow,' I said thoughtfully, 'during the lunch break, could you bring along the original court file? There may be a few documents that were not sent with the summons.'

'Not a problem, sir. But, instead of my coming, would it be all right if you sent your *munshi*, your legal clerk, Hetram? I'll put it into a polythene bag. Then if Hetram can return it to me when you are done with it. Before the end of the day…'

'Let's do it like that,' I agreed. I peeled out another two thousand rupees and gave it to him.

This time he took the money without any reluctance. He knew he was going out of his way. 'Anything else?'

'Yes,' I said. 'When is the next hearing?'

'In two weeks from now.'

'The thing is, Gopal Ram,' I said, 'I want to delay this case by another three months.'

'But on this hearing,' he said, looking anxious, 'the judge will see my report and send the police.'

'There is a solution,' I said to him. 'Disappear the file.'

Just as Lord Patel's son was disappeared, I thought to myself.

He laughed at the suggestion. 'You are very clever, sir. That can be fixed.'

The file would be untraceable at the next hearing. The judge would shout at his staff to track it down, but then, despite his anger, when nothing was found he'd just adjourn it again.

More money unfurled its wings. I gave Gopal an advance, which he graciously accepted, and I promised him the rest once I was convinced that the file had been disappeared for a week. He withdrew from my house, smiling from ear to ear.

Singhania and Kapoor's junior lawyers, who were chasing the case at this moment – their seniors being too busy arguing cases before five-member benches of the Supreme Court – didn't find the case listed before the competent court when they came the next day, and when these bright young lads enquired they were told that there was simply no petition. 'Maybe it has been lost somewhere,' one of the clerks working in the Registry said to them. 'Come tomorrow.' So tomorrow and tomorrow, the days rolled by, and then finally, when one week was over, the file reappeared.

I don't know how Singhania and Kapoor fobbed Patel off, but this is really what happened. Their juniors wouldn't know the first thing about how the system in the Thirty Thousand Courts works. It's not such an easy matter to prosecute a lawyer from the same courts. But it's not only in the Thirty Thousand Courts that corruption is rife – it's all over the country.

* * *

Court clerk corruption is widespread and practically a universal phenomenon in hundreds of subordinate courts all over India. Years ago, when I joined the Bar, within a few months of commencing practice at the subordinate courts in the capital I observed some colleagues, shortly before court hours began, getting their ten-rupee notes changed into two-rupee notes. These notes, I had learnt by then, would be required for 'assistance' from clerks in the courts and other judicial departments. The rate has since been hiked up, owing to inflationary measures, to fifty rupees for most petty jobs.

Money must be paid to the court clerk for every small thing, such as finding out a date, having a rent voucher prepared, filing a process fee for the service of summons, getting an application listed the next day – the list is interminable. Nothing moves without money. So much so that these small transactions are accepted as standard practice, and many court clerks have come to feel and behave as if it is their right and due. Money is paid by the litigant, the lawyer or the lawyer's clerk as a matter of routine and without a thought – many of them have ceased to think of it as a bribe.

A businessman such as Lord Patel understands that the balance sheet does not always accurately reflect the health of the company. So also there is a difference between what economists might call 'real income' and what is stated in the books. The salaries of these court clerks are substantially supplemented by means of these 'daily wages', and in certain cases such net monthly takings may well be more than the actual salaries earned.

The amount paid to a court functionary varies with the nature of the task assigned. On a particular occasion, my *munshi*, Hetram, gave a twenty-rupee note to a process server – the court functionary who delivers summonses to witnesses and parties – to get a certain service of summons effected. The *pyada* – the 'chess pawn', as this court emissary is known – looked at him in mock sorrow and said, '*Munshi-ji*, you can forget my going to Janakpuri. For twenty rupees I am not even willing to go home.'

* * *

When Hetram brought over the original case file the following day, I found attached to the complaint a list of witnesses and a statement by Balram, the security guard at the White House, as I had suspected. His deposition spoke clearly and unambiguously about the threat I had made to his master. I smiled to myself.

The case Patel had filed against me wasn't making any progress. His American-trained lawyers had finally wised up to the situation and insisted with the judge that there were far too many delays occurring on account of my not being served with the summons, and that the police should be required to serve the summons instead. So yes, when instead of my friend Gopal Ram, the police turned up a few months later – as we had both anticipated – I realised it was finally time to show up in the courtroom.

Patel's American-trained lawyer brats were out to milk him for his money's worth, and he probably recognised that, but as money's no object for someone like him, he had decided to file this case against me. And he had a witness. One witness, but an important one.

Someone who would testify that I had threatened his son Amit.

It was Balram, the security guard, at whom I had shouted threats against Amit the day I was detained at Daryaganj Police Station and interrogated about the death of Sunil Gupta. It was after my release that, in a sudden flash of awareness, I had first suspected Amit was involved in my sister's death.

In the criminal complaint mechanism, the complainant, in this case Lord Patel, has to convince the court a prima facie case exists against the accused, namely myself in this case. So he has to produce a witness and get him to make a statement on oath implicating the accused.

Balram had already been examined on oath by Lord Patel's lawyers and he had made a statement against me, which I had read over several times. I noticed that the second security guard, who had been sympathetic to me, had chosen not to make any statement. So there was just a single witness for me to discredit.

Now that I was going to appear in court, Balram would have to reappear in court and repeat what he had said earlier, but I would then have an opportunity to cross-examine him. Afterwards, I would have the chance to produce my own witnesses, if any.

3

Word had spread in the Thirty Thousand Courts that a lawyer was being charged in the Amit Patel kidnap case, so there was quite a crowd milling around the courtroom that day. Mostly lawyers, but some members of the press as well. It hadn't yet become a big media story, possibly because nothing had actually happened. That is to say, no case had taken off against me. It was all very preliminary. But today was crucial. Half a dozen cameramen stood outside the courtroom, but they were not as yet aware who they needed to photograph apart from the great Lord Patel himself, so I slipped in, unnoticed.

Aware of the importance of the case, the Sessions Judge dealing with the case, a man with the face of a smiling pig, was nattily attired in spanking new robes. He was clearly enjoying the media attention. As for myself, I was wearing a black coat that I had picked up the previous week from a roadside vendor in Connaught Place, who sells some excellent new-looking, but second-hand, clothes that come in from overseas that are sold for a fraction of the price they would cost in a regular store at the mall. This particular coat had caught my attention because of the fine material and new appearance. Later, when I examined the label, I discovered to my amusement it was actually a fireman's uniform from far-off Edinburgh. It didn't matter, though I took care to tear out the label.

Singhania and Kapoor's Harvard- and Yale-trained lawyers were wearing special tailored outfits from a well-known shop in Connaught Place that bragged of being 'bespoke tailors', whatever that meant. There were two of them. The senior of the pair parted his hair in the centre and the other one had curly hair.

Centre Parting and Curly Hair were busy whispering to each other and Lord Patel. Discussing case strategy. Really, I thought, was there so much to discuss?

Lord Patel himself was dressed impressively in a Savile Row suit, the original genuine bespoke tailoring, the shop's label discreetly exposed, a green bow fluttering in the draught from an open window. His son might have disappeared, but appearances needed to be maintained, I supposed. He looked at me with anger from time to time, his eyes burning like coals. As for the court audience, their eyes were all fixed on Lord Patel. Perhaps I wasn't very impressive as a villain. Not the handsome young thug with rippling muscles and a black curled moustache that they might have liked to see.

It was the second time I was meeting the British-born billionaire in the flesh; our first encounter had been far from pleasant. He did look a bit the worse for wear, and I imagined he had added a few pounds since the previous occasion.

Lord Patel would qualify as a fat man, but only just. He was not obscenely fat, but he could not be called only a little plump. He was a normally fat man. In his youth he had been good-looking; there was still a slimmer, almost handsome face hiding behind the now fleshy countenance. Thick eyebrows, narrow alert eyes radiated a keen intelligence. A couple of extra chins, no more.

I was in my mid-forties, he was closer to the mid-century mark; we both had grizzled hair, his receding more than mine. I flattered myself that I looked a decade younger than him.

'*Case bulao*,' the judge instructed the court crier. 'Call out the case.'

The court crier's job is simply to go outside the courtroom and bellow out the case name and number so that if any interested party is in the vicinity he can come rushing in. The grey-uniformed man passed by us all, stood outside the courtroom and gave a great shout in the manner of a vegetable trader hawking potatoes.

'*Bara sau bees* number,' he yelled. 'Case number twelve hundred and twenty. Lard Patel' – I smothered a laugh – 'versus Ramesh Kumar.'

We all drew closer to the judge then – Lord Patel, his lawyers and myself. Balram stayed a bit behind. As a lawyer, I had the option of either representing myself in this case or getting one of my colleagues to act for me. It's generally considered advisable to have someone else represent you – that is the conventional wisdom – but this case was different and I had decided to represent myself.

'Okay,' said the judge. 'Let's get started. Please call your witness. How many are you calling?'

'Only two, sir,' Centre Parting said. 'That should be enough. We have a simple and easy case.'

'Call your witness,' said the judge noncommittally.

The first witness was a court clerk who appeared with the records of a case I had previously filed against Amit Patel seeking his eviction from the White House.

The statement was over in a matter of minutes.

'I have brought the original case records,' this witness said. 'Yes, there is a *vakalatnama*, the letter of authority in favour of a lawyer. Yes, the case has been filed by one Ramesh Kumar.' And, in reply to a question from Curly as to what had been the consequences, he answered competently that Amit Patel had been successfully evicted from the premises.

'Are you Ramesh Kumar?' the judge asked me once the witness had finished giving his statement.

'Yes, Your Honour.'

'The very Ramesh Kumar who filed the petition that has been brought to the court?'

'The very same one,' I said.

I heard supportive laughter in the court. The lawyers from the Thirty Thousand Courts were behind me, even if no one else was.

'Your witness,' said the judge.

'No need, Your Honour. These are all matters of record.'

'Call the next witness,' the judge instructed.

And now it was paunchy, sloppy Balram's turn to show up; only he wasn't as sloppy today. He was wearing the usual security guard's uniform but it was crisply ironed and starched. He came up in a brisk manner, confidently enough. Singhania and Kapoor first conducted their examination-in-chief, and like a parrot trained many times over he spoke of my arrival at the gates of the White House in a taxi and the threats I had issued against Amit Patel. He was smooth, too smooth, I thought, and I detected something amiss there.

'Your witness,' Centre Parting said.

I stepped forward.

'You have just said on oath,' I said, 'that I came to the White House and threatened your master. Is that correct?'

'It is correct,' he said. 'And you very well know this is what you did.'

He was being polite, but wouldn't be for much longer.

'What was my threat?'

'You would evict him, kidnap him and kill him.'

'All three things, eh?' I smiled. 'If you have such a good memory, can you tell me the colour of the shirt I was wearing?'

'It was . . .' He paused, trying to remember. 'It was blue.'

'And was I wearing a coat? A lawyer's coat?'

'I don't think so.'

'Was it a working day?'

'I was working.'

'That was not my question. You work even on Sundays. But the day when I came, was it a working day?'

'Yes, it was. It was a Tuesday.'

'Do you know my profession?'

'Yes, you are a lawyer.'

'So wouldn't I be wearing a lawyer's coat on a working day – assuming that I was working?'

'Maybe.'

'Maybe,' I said. 'Maybe not.' I turned towards my colleagues momentarily. 'He is not sure.' I turned to face him again. 'So you are not sure.'

'I am not sure.' He looked disconcerted now.

'You are not sure whether I was wearing a coat, but are certain that I was wearing a blue shirt?' I allowed myself a small laugh. 'How can this be?'

He was quiet.

And then I said, very politely: 'I put it to you that you are speaking an untruth when you say you remember I was wearing a blue shirt.'

'I am not sure,' he muttered. I could see he was sweating.

'You have said in your statement I came in a taxi – is that correct?'

'That is right. You were in a taxi.'

'Can you tell me the number of the taxi?'

'I did not note the number.'

'What kind of security guard are you?' I said, a bit loudly. 'Don't you note the numbers of the cars that come to visit your master?'

Lord Patel was taking little prancing steps up and down, whispering into his lawyers' ears. I could understand his tension, the excitement and the pain he was experiencing at that moment. The butterfly continued to dance around his buttoned-up shirt, but, inside, the man's heart trembled. And why wouldn't it? He was after all standing next to the man he had accused of kidnapping and possibly murdering his son.

'Your Honour, our witness is being intimidated,' Curly Hair said.

'I think that is a reasonable question, and there is no intimidation,' ruled the judge. He turned to the witness. 'Answer the question.'

'We note the numbers of the cars that we allow to enter the White House,' said the guard. 'In your case, you were sent back. We never allowed you to enter.'

'But,' I said, 'you say that I threatened your master. Did I abuse him as well?'

'Yes,' he said. 'You called him a . . .'

'Yes, yes.'

'You called him a *madarchod*, a motherfucker.'

A couple of lawyers behind me sniggered.

'So if according to you I threatened your master, and if according to you I abused him, called him' – a pause – 'a motherfucker' – more sniggers – 'then did you not think it appropriate to write down the number of the taxi in your register?'

He was silent.

I took a well-calculated risk in asking this question. I had no idea at all if he had noted the number of the taxi. But I surmised, had he done so, he wouldn't have been the sole witness appearing in court. They would have traced the taxi, given the taxi driver a pile of cash, and got him to testify against me in court. Surely. It was therefore clear to me that the taxi's number had not been noted.

'Answer my question,' I said.

'I forgot,' he said sullenly.

'You forgot,' I repeated. 'You forgot to note down the number of the car, and you forgot what clothes I was wearing, whether I was dressed or not, but – but you remember my face.'

'I remember your face very well,' he said grimly, having decided to take an aggressive stance now.

'Okay,' I said. 'Let me jog your memory just a little bit more. Can you tell me what the weather was like on that day?'

'It was a warm day,' he said.

'Everyone knows that July is warm,' I said, 'but was it cloudy?'

'No,' he said. 'It was a clear sky.'

'I put it to you that it was a cloudy day.'

'No.' He was insistent.

I pulled out a sheaf of papers from inside a plastic file, and gave it to the judge. A copy to Curly Hair and Centre Parting. Lord Patel bustled up to study it.

'This is the weather report that appeared the following day' I said. Met Department Weather Report: "Cloudy conditions to continue with rain forecast for the evening".' I turned to the witness. 'All right, Balram, the court now knows the weather that day. Now don't tell us any more lies. I have two more questions. Can you describe to us the face of the taxi driver?'

'I don't remember.'

Lord Patel's face was red with anger. The witness was not performing well at all. The security guard had possibly never been called as a witness in a criminal court before. I suspected that he was drinking on duty, possibly stealing stuff from Amit's larder, because I recalled his slurred speech on the day of my encounter with him. He couldn't remember the clothes I had been wearing that day, the number plate of the taxi I had taken to the house, the face of the taxi driver, or even whether it had been a sunny or a cloudy day. I suspected that he was an alcoholic, and that partly explained his slovenly attire and demeanour.

'One last question. Mr Balram. Are you fond of drinking?'

'I take a drink sometimes,' he said. 'Never while on duty.'

'I put it to you that you were drunk the day I came to the White House.'

'That's a lie.' He was panting with anger.

'I put it to you that you cannot remember the weather, the clothes I was wearing, or anything that I said to you because you were drunk. And I suggest to you that you have even taken a drink or two before coming to the court. Will you submit to a breathalyser test?'

'You are a liar,' he shouted, beside himself with anger. 'I did not drink before and I have not drunk today. I don't need to take any test.'

'Behave yourself in my courtroom,' shouted the judge. 'You don't have to shout.'

The witness immediately quietened down.

'Judge *saab*, I am being insulted, abused,' he said with an aggrieved air. 'I am sorry.'

'Any more questions, counsel?

'No more questions, Your Honour.'

The witness retreated shamefaced.

I hoped this would be the end of the matter, but I knew better than to be confident of that. Lord Patel looked far from defeated. He still had a semi-triumphant expression on his face as if he had already fixed the verdict. And the judge, too, while appearing neutral, was possibly only being political; he knew the courtroom was full of lawyers who were watching him. Judges too could be purchased.

'. . . from your side?'

I came out of my reverie. Unbelievably, the judge was asking me if I intended to produce any witnesses.

'I believe I have discredited the witness sufficiently,' I said. 'I haven't asked for a breath test, but if Your Honour is not satisfied that he is not a reliable witness, I ask that he be subjected to a breath test.'

'That is not relevant, counsel,' said the judge.

I heard whispers behind me. The lawyers were realising that the man before them had sold out. There were loud whispers and mutterings. 'Manipur High Court ruling,' one lawyer sniggered to another. Someone laughed. We all knew what it meant. In these corrupt precincts, it was often said, when you couldn't persuade a judge with precedents drawn from the verdicts of the Supreme Court and various High Courts, there was a north-eastern court whose verdicts always helped judges see the point: Manipur. Or Moneypur.

'Your Honour would not like to send him for a test,' I said, smiling.

'It is not necessary,' he insisted.

'And Your Honour is also not satisfied that I have managed to discredit his testimony.'

'I am not satisfied,' he said. 'I believe that you have shown he has a poor memory. But he has been very clear you came to the White House, where Lord Patel's son lived, and' – he actually cast a servile look in his benefactor's direction at this point; there was no doubt remaining in my mind that Lord Patel had greased both his palms and his feet as well – 'and threatened and abused Amit Patel.'

'I see,' I said evenly. 'In that case, I would like to have the opportunity to produce witnesses in support of my defence.'

'All right,' he said, looking at the clock. 'It's getting towards lunchtime now. Can we do this after the break? Singhania and Kapoor – is that okay with you?'

'Oh, yes, Your Honour.'

The lawyers were grinning from ear to ear. I thought one of them would poke out his tongue at me. Your goose has been cooked, their expressions seemed to say, and we are going to enjoy hot soup very soon before we start to savour your flesh.

As for the judge himself, he was unable to look me in the face any more, and had dropped any signs of pretence. It was clear, his body language indicated, that he would rule against me. He didn't have much faith that I could defend myself successfully.

4

When we resumed after the recess, the courtroom was packed. Even the corridor was full of lawyers. It was as if a World Cup final were in progress, with India playing Pakistan.

Lord Patel, Curly Hair and Centre Parting were already there when I entered. This time the photojournalists knew who I was, and clicked away. It would be front-page news tomorrow. Amit Patel's disappearance had been covered by all the major newspapers and television channels, but the news had died down after a few weeks. There is only so much you can write about someone who has disappeared. The police made statements that they were investigating the case, but had not named me as a possible suspect. As for the complaint case filed against me by Lord Patel, they hadn't wanted to give it much publicity, so no one even knew about it until my appearance in court today.

I suspected it would make bigger headlines if the case against me was formally registered. It would then be a major running story until I was either acquitted or convicted. But I wasn't about to allow them even to charge me.

The judge might not have enjoyed his lunch, for the piggish smile was gone, replaced by a scowl. As soon as he had seated himself, he assumed a tough, businesslike demeanour, looking at me as if he had already convicted me.

'Call your witnesses,' he said rudely.

'I've provided him with the list,' I said, pointing to the court crier.

'Hari Singh, *pesh ho*!' the court attendant bellowed.

Hari Singh entered. He was a tall, sturdy fellow, who had his shirt out and a cloth over his shoulder as if he were still at the restaurant where he worked serving customers.

'Your name and profession?' I prompted him.

'My name is Hari Singh, father's name Lal Singh. I work in a restaurant close to the courts as a waiter.'

'Are you happy with your job?'

'*Arre, saab*, someone like you comes over, enjoys lunch and leaves a tip, we poor fellows manage somehow, but most people don't leave anything at all. And the owner doesn't pay us a fair wage. It's difficult in these times to manage.'

'Do you know a place in south Delhi called the White House?'

'*Arre, saab*, that's the place we went to a year ago, isn't it? That security guard misbehaved with you, and didn't allow you to enter . . .'

'Okay,' I said. 'Tell the court what happened that day.'

Hari Singh proceeded to fluently recount the events of that day. He, together with me and a man called Sikander, had gone to the White House in a taxi. I had promised both of them there were possibilities for getting jobs there, Hari Singh as a waiter and Sikander as a gardener. The establishment might have need for a trained waiter to serve food at the dining table as well as an additional gardener to tend the spacious lawns of the White House (so I had advised them). It was a warm, cloudy day and there was a lot of traffic on the streets. We were coming from the courts. I had taken time off work to give them both personal introductions. I told them I needed to meet Amit Patel anyhow, and once I had introduced them they could vamoose and I would stay and chat with Amit. Amit was a friend, I had told them.

'What happened,' I asked, 'when we reached the White House?'

'We were stopped by a drunken security guard who wouldn't allow the taxi to enter.'

'Would you recognise the man if you saw him again?'

'*Mota tha*,' he said, hesitantly. 'He was a paunchy fellow, I remember, but this was a long while ago and I'm not sure I would.'

'All right, Hari Singh,' I said. 'Can you look around the courtroom right now and tell me if you see him anywhere?'

Hari Singh looked around and saw the uniformed security guard sitting on one of the chairs.

'That's him, sir,' he said. 'That's the fellow.'

'*Jhooth bol ra hai saala*,' shouted Balram. 'That scumbag is lying.'

'*Behenchod*! Sisterfucker!' Hari Singh yelled back. 'Call me a liar and I will rape your mother.'

'Quiet, quiet,' shouted the judge. 'Be quiet the both of you, or else I'll be sending you to the lock-up.'

Singhania and Kapoor tried very hard to discredit the witness but they couldn't manage it. Hari Singh was just too smooth for them. He peppered his answers with sharp humour that got him more than a couple of laughs from the court audience.

* * *

'Your name and occupation please.' I was examining my second witness.

'I am Sikander Ahmed and I work at Delhi University as a gardener.'

'How do you know me?'

'I know you through your sister, sir. She used to teach at the university, God bless her departed soul.'

'Did you accompany me almost a year ago to the White House?'

'I am about to retire from the university, and we hardly get any pension. I had gone to your house to ask you if you knew anyone who could provide me with a job. You asked me to come to the courts one day and you would take me to the White House, where there might be a chance for me to get a job. Three of us were together — the man who came before, your good self and myself.'

'All right,' I said. 'Tell me what happened that day.'

Sikander Ahmed began to recount with minor variations – I had been through each variation innumerable times carefully – more or less the same tale that shortly before had unfolded from the lips of the smooth-talking waiter. As he spoke, I glanced at the judge, who was looking very, very uncomfortable with this turn of events, and also at Patel and Centre Parting, who were conferring urgently while Curly Hair listened to the testimony. Across the room, I heard the words 'High Court' and 'Supreme Court'. I could guess what was troubling Centre Parting. I could bet on what was troubling the Sessions Judge.

'Your witness.' I turned to Curly Hair, who came forward diffidently, all swagger gone.

You can gain some idea of how easily a witness can be intimidated from his testimony, to bring out contradictions and to discredit him in general. Singhania and Kapoor had failed to discredit Hari Singh and they didn't think they would be able to do so with Sikander Ahmed either, who had spoken throughout in a composed and convincing manner.

Curly Hair went through the motions, but it was clear their case would be thrown out.

The judge knew, were he still to attempt to prosecute me, the media was in attendance and would report the verdict adversely, and my appeal to the High Court and thereafter to the Supreme Court if need be would almost certainly be accepted. That's what Centre Parting was trying to explain to Lord Patel.

'Is Your Honour going to continue with this case?' I looked him squarely in the eye, almost daring him to say 'Yes'. He'd been paid to turn grey into white or black as the case may be, but even he knew that he lacked the power or authority to turn white into black.

He turned his gaze away from me and didn't bother to look at Lord Patel – a punctured, deflated version of his former strutting self – or his anxious lawyers who were still, amazingly enough, pleading with him to take the case forward.

'Steno, please type out,' said the judge, '"After hearing the evidence I have come to the conclusion that no prima facie case has been established to merit further investigations." Case dismissed.' He stood up and left.

A cheer went out from the audience, the main thrust of that cheer coming from my brethren in law, who saw that day, unusually perhaps, justice being done in the Thirty Thousand Courts.

Part Three
Breakfast

5

May I offer you a glass of water, Lord Patel? I must not be remiss in my duties as a host. Oh, you've already had some. Well, let me pour myself a small cup from the *surahi*. An unusual item to find in a lawyer's chambers, isn't it? Apart from the fact that I like its delicate shape, the reason I store drinking water in this earthen vessel is because it keeps the water just cool enough for my taste. Not too cold or too warm, you see. You get the fragrance of the earth as well.

The disadvantage, of course, is that your clients may wonder if you are perhaps so poor that you cannot afford a fridge. Also, some insect or creature seeking respite from the heat might decide to crawl inside. Possibly even a snake. Don't worry. You have drunk from this cistern, but do not worry. You won't find any snakes crawling about the premises of the Thirty Thousand Courts, unless they are of the human variety – and those, I'm sorry to say, you will find aplenty. You smile. No, sir – I am being perfectly serious.

Do you prefer tea or coffee? Tea? Same as me. Let us have a cup before we continue this conversation. I'm sorry, I don't have any fancy silverware – you'll have to make do with milky tea served in a thick, corrugated glass, the kind your drivers may drink from. Is that all right with you? Splendid. Well then, Hetram will go and tell one of the stall owners just outside the court to send over two special teas.

My sister Ruhno loved coffee. She sometimes had tea just to keep me company, but it was coffee that she really liked. You wish to commiserate with me for the death of my sister? Ah, yes, it was the most terrible thing to have happened. She was so young. And we had this very special relationship, my sister and I. You see, Lord Patel, I began to work in the Thirty Thousand Courts because I needed to support an ailing father, who had been diagnosed with skin cancer, a mother who did not keep very well at the time either, and a much younger sister; when I began my law practice, I was twenty-eight and she was eight.

My father had been ill for some years. There wasn't enough money to pay the fees for my last year at college, so I had to give tuitions and do other odd jobs. I was studying law – which in India is a course that is not difficult to gain admission to – but it was not my first preference; I would've preferred to study English literature. Of course I was interested in literature from all parts of the world, from Russia and France in particular, but in India, as a former colonised country, we study all these other literatures under the rubric of English literature.

My father, who worked as a clerk in a nationalised insurance company, was not too dictatorial, but he was poorly – we were to realise only later that at that stage the cancer was already present though dormant – and he impressed upon me the need to choose a subject at university that would provide me with some kind of guaranteed employment. He wanted me to study accountancy and commerce, his point being that there would never, as long as trade and business existed, be a surfeit of accountants or bookkeepers.

If there was one subject in the world I detested, it was accountancy, and, even though I could see my father's line of reasoning, I explained that it was something I had an aversion to. He was disappointed, of course, but he perked up when I mentioned that the study of law, the second choice he had suggested, was something I could not only deal with but also be interested in. Of course, at the time, in my youthful idealism, I imagined that the study of law had something to do with justice!

You laugh. Do not laugh, please. You see, I was not so naïve as to not know there is a great deal of injustice in the world, and that courts too sometimes seal their approval on an act of injustice. This much I was aware of, but I had no conception, you see, of the scale or level of injustice – the mockery of everything we had been taught at university.

Your laughter tells me that despite your travels and businesses in different continents, despite your knowledge of the corruption and injustice that exist in many countries, you still do not really understand what goes on here, in India, in the name of justice. Neither did I, and I was a well-read person for my generation, as someone who has a passion for literature is likely to be.

I was given a clue on the very first day I walked about the corridors of the Thirty Thousand Courts in my newly acquired lawyer's tie, coat and gown. I overheard two grey-haired lawyers, a thin one and a fat one, arguing, and paused to overhear their remarks. Towards the end of their discussion, the thin, spindly lawyer with a full shock of grey hair mournfully told the other one how there was no justice in the courts. And this so enraged the other lawyer, as your amused reaction has angered me somewhat, that he told his colleague in plain words he should drop his attitude of British understatement – the hell with it, he should say it plainly as it was. 'Every day, my friend,' he said, holding the other with a steely gaze. 'Every day,' he repeated for dramatic effect, 'and every hour of every working day, justice is being fucked in these courtrooms.'

* * *

As I said, my father developed skin cancer. The doctors told us it had been diagnosed quite early, and the chances of his survival were high. The cancer started on his face, and then slowly, inexorably, began to move downwards. At times it seemed he was improving. In fact, after about five months, the doctors declared him cured. We were all delighted with the news and celebrated with a sumptuous meal at the Moti Mahal restaurant on Daryaganj, and later that night, when we got home, my father and I even uncorked a bottle of Golconda wine. This will tell you that, despite my father's humble position as a clerk in the General Insurance Company, we were not your typical conservative middle-class family, but had a modern Westernised slant to our upbringing, and held aspirations to a grander status. History repeats itself, you see. My father had, in his youth, hopes of becoming a singer in Bollywood, but retreated to safer pastures after five or six years of struggle in the industry.

Our festivity didn't last long, for hardly a few weeks later he began to experience the recurrence of certain troubling symptoms, and when we took him to the government hospital, we were told by a sad-looking oncologist that it was unexpected bad news, but yes, there could be no doubt about it, the cancer had returned.

My father stopped going to the office now, as his body could no longer bear the stress of a nine-to-five routine, but even in this state of ill health he remained active and earned money for the day-to-day expenses of running a household – the pension he was receiving being barely adequate to pay the electricity and water bills. From being a clerk in a nationalised insurance company, he turned to being an insurance agent, and once or twice a week, overruling all protests from my mother and sister, he would head off in an auto-rickshaw or bus to go and get some person insured. The family was distressed, and I was under pressure to take over financial responsibility for the family, but I still had a few weeks to wait for my law examination results to be announced. It was in many ways ironic, wasn't it, for my father to be selling life insurance to people at a time when his own life would soon come to an end.

Finally, my examination results were declared. I passed, got myself registered at the Delhi Bar Council and became a qualified lawyer, all in a matter of a few days. I began to practise law at the Thirty Thousand Courts, where I could hope to start earning some money right from the beginning.

Two months after I began visiting the courts, my father became confined to the house at first and then increasingly to his bed. Despite the further chemotherapy sessions, the disease began to spread. In six months it had reached his stomach. We had to have him hospitalised at that juncture, and a tube was inserted into his stomach. He was fed through that tube and he remained in that bed for another six months; then one day, to our sadness and relief – which was the greater, it was difficult to say – he passed away.

It wasn't the cancer that killed my father. It was the chemotherapy. I have learnt subsequently that is quite often the case.

The relatives all came and condoled with us, and everyone told me the responsibility now fell on my shoulders. As if I didn't know that already. Some of my father's colleagues from the General Insurance Company came to attend the *chautha*, the ceremony held on the fourth day, and they told me they would help me get a job in the firm as a clerk. A case could be put up to the divisional manager, if I was interested. Some colleagues including my father's boss came to attend the *terveen*, the ceremony held on the thirteenth day. Mr Gupta, manager of the General Insurance Company branch where my father had worked, directly asked me if I wished to work at the desk where my father had slaved for more than twenty years. But I was not interested. Me, a clerk? Not on your life. The life of a lawyer, even one who was based in the Thirty Thousand Courts, was a hundred times preferable.

Meanwhile, at the courts I filled in forms, deposited traffic fines on behalf of clients, and did all kinds of petty work just so I could bring home some money. For we were broke, badly broke.

But for all that, we muddled along, the three of us: my mother, my sister and me. Until the time the second tragedy struck, barely two years after my father's death. For some months now, my mother had felt strange sensations in her throat, difficulty swallowing, and we had all kinds of tests done on her, but they showed up nothing. 'It's probably indigestion,' said one of the doctors, and we went away satisfied – only to return a month later when the problem resurfaced in an aggravated form. Eventually things became so bad that she couldn't swallow any food, and this time when we took her to the hospital, the tests did show up something: cancer of the pancreas. Within months she too was dead.

* * *

Ah, the *mathis* and *fains* have arrived. And hot mugs of tea as well. Please start, Lord Patel.

You are not hungry, you say. Do try a *fain* at least. They are very light. The *fain*, allow me to inform you, is something like an Indian version of the French croissant, but it is unheard of outside the subcontinent, and even here in this country it is eaten mostly by poor people. Unlike the croissant and its many variants, which can be taken with butter and jam, or baked with a filling of raisins, cream or chocolate, our Indian substitute is without such accompaniments. Healthier, though, wouldn't you say?

Ah, you'll try one. Good.

* * *

The month my mother died, a murder case came my way. One of my associates, a man called Bihari, sent it to me. It involved a young student at the university who had stabbed his roommate. The father came down from Patna, and Bihari befriended him in the courts. It was difficult to resist Bihari. A murder case involving the son of a wealthy farmer from Bihar obviously meant quite a lot of money. A lawyer joked that I could now sell off my old scooter and buy one of the smart small cars that had recently begun to be advertised. But I decided to send Ruhno to boarding school instead.

Why did I send my beloved sister to a hill station that was at least a day's journey from New Delhi, you will doubtless want to know. Well, you see, she was at that age where it's not right for her to stay with a man, even if that man happens to be her brother. This is not only the way I think, I assure you. Quite often our courts – the ones dealing with matrimonial cases in which questions of child custody come up – think similarly. The custody of a young girl is awarded to the mother because the girl is at that tender age just on the brink of womanhood. From a bud, she becomes a flower. And in this blossoming phase of her life, it is best that she is with other older women, rather than with a crusty old bachelor such as myself.

Ruhno blossomed in Shimla, but even after she had finished school and become a young woman, I thought it best for her to continue with her college education in Shimla.

You've seen my sister. You know she was beautiful. I too have chiselled features like her, but the Almighty forgot to slap some plaster on the bones. In her case, though, he patted flesh at the right places, down to her perfectly shaped lips, the dimple in her soft, round cheeks whenever she smiled, the sparkle of her white teeth whenever she laughed. At five foot two, my sister was a full head shorter than I am, but I'm the tall one; she was never considered short, at least by Indian standards. Do you know what made her more beautiful? It was the grace inherent in all her movements. She never wished to learn to dance, despite my mother egging her on, but every movement of hers was imbued with some kind of natural grace. Again, of the two of us, I was the ungainly, awkward one, although, God bless her soul, she always looked up to me as her moral and intellectual superior. Till her reason got corrupted, that is to say.

I've mentioned to you already how I always wanted to study literature, but gave in to family pressure to study a subject more likely to lead to a job, or at least an income. When it came to my sister's time to go to university, I was certain she would want to study literature, as she had always been fond of reading, and when she grew older we would often discuss books we had both read. I was in for a bit of a surprise. She wanted to study commerce – the subject that my father had hoped I would study and against which I had rebelled!

Anyhow, I'm a great believer in letting people follow careers of their own choosing, so after the initial shock I told her to go ahead and apply to take a bachelor's degree in commerce from Bede's College, Shimla, where because of her excellent school results she was certain to gain admission. She did her bachelor's degree in the subject, and after that she went on to do a master's degree, and then when I asked her if she would like to look for employment in private companies she said she wanted to do her PhD in commerce. A PhD? And that too in commerce! For a while I was mystified by her decision and speculated whether there was a boy in Shimla she was interested in, who could be the reason for her to want to stay on in university. But I finally understood she liked the life of an academic, and didn't really want to work in a private company. It takes all kinds to make the world, I guess, and this was my very own beloved sister.

I have to say here that Ruhno's decision to do a PhD in commerce convinced me she lacked a certain kind of emotional intelligence. I wouldn't make this statement if someone wanted to do a PhD in management sciences or even economics . . . but commerce? Don't ask me to explain why. Perhaps it's just prejudice on my part.

In a way, it was good she studied in Himachal, because most people in that northern hill state are simple and trustworthy people, unlike the people in Delhi – even though it is the city I was born in and a city that I love. Each time I caught the *Himalayan Queen* from Shimla via Kalka back to Delhi, I would notice the difference as soon as the train careened into New Delhi railway station and the red-tunicked porters rushed to carry my bags for me, and minutes later when the taxi drivers tried to persuade me to engage their services for a price that was generally three or even four times the standard fare. They would approach their customer with a kind of swagger, their facial expressions and body language suggestive of a pantomime or an act that screamed out to anyone who understood it, 'I am going to cheat you, my friend', and, unless you knew how to neutralise their attack by some kind of reverse pantomime, they would not give up on you. The simple Himachalis, and my Ruhno was one of them, were a world apart. Perhaps it was good, I told myself sometimes, that Ruhno studied in that hill town for all those years. On the other hand, I sometimes wondered if it had been a bad decision, because it kept her sheltered from the real world that she would have to face up to sooner or later, and it kept her judgement of people in general poor and underdeveloped.

While she studied in Shimla and I practised law at the Thirty Thousand Courts, I made sure that all her needs were met, gave her as generous an allowance as my earnings permitted, and kept in touch with her on an almost daily basis. I also visited her frequently.

I would probably have visited my sister as often as I did in any case, but I have to admit that Shimla's natural surroundings were an added attraction. You see, Lord Patel, the apartment I live in is part of a housing co-operative, in which my father took membership, and which was designed to cater to the needs and budget of lower-middle-class households. We had a two-bedroom apartment on the third floor, and there are about three hundred similar apartments all around – some with an extra storeroom, some an extra study, some with a garage, some without – built quite close to each other, with narrow streets and alleyways between them. And, just to pay lip-service to having a bit of greenery around, there are three small parks that have been created nearby as well.

Ruhno returned to live with me barely three years ago once she had finished her studies. In the first year or so after her return, Ruhno was mostly at home or in one of the libraries inside Delhi University. She took great care of me and of the house. Our parents' photo was framed and left to hang in the main living room, surrounded with fresh marigold flowers.

She had a storeroom converted into a prayer room containing statues of various gods and goddesses. The house was falling apart, and Ruhno took great interest in its refurbishment – something I had had no time to pay attention to. Once a week we went to see a movie at one of the new multiplexes. Her nature was so warm and friendly that she was never short of company. The neighbours liked her, the relatives who lived close by now dropped in more often, and she struck up several friendships with research scholars whom she met in the university's libraries. My sister was sociable, more sociable than me at any rate, and very conscious of keeping up connections with the extended family, which I personally never cared for. I should also mention here perhaps that among her many good qualities was something found less commonly in the middle class: she was always very respectful to the lower class and the underprivileged, never bossy or ordering them about. She had excellent manners, and the feminine side to her personality made their display seem yet more graceful.

Once in a while some former class fellows from college or school in Shimla happened to visit Delhi, and then she took them around the city, or invited them home for lunch or dinner. She was occupied, but at the same time she was free. Free enough to wait for me to return from court, heat up water for a bath, make a cup of tea for me and listen patiently to me rambling on about the events of the day. Free enough even to cook certain dishes that worked better on a slow fire. For these culinary experiments, she used a special kind of charcoal stove gifted to her by a friend who'd travelled to Japan. It wasn't only meats in the American barbecue style that she rustled up, but all kinds of delectable vegetable dishes as well as magnificent desserts.

All this was to change the day Ruhno landed a job as a lecturer at Delhi University. She had started applying for jobs seriously once she had finished her PhD thesis and a leading academic publisher had agreed to publish it. A couple of interviews followed, and soon she was offered a post in the Faculty of Management. Although her new job made great demands on her, she did not neglect the home front and still had time for me.

Once Ruhno began teaching at the university, and her colleagues became aware that her brother was a lawyer, the occasional piece of work came my way. As you appreciate yourself, Lord Patel, this is how a law practice operates all over the world: through referral, because people know someone you happen to know.

6

India is changing, you remarked to me on the day I met you just one year ago. I had gone to talk to you about the relationship that was developing between your son and my sister.

Yes, indeed, you are right, Lord Patel. India is changing, but not all of us are changing at the same pace. Some slower, some faster. As a Bollywood actress remarked recently in an interview with the BBC, India lives in several centuries at the same time.

One of my college friends, Prem Sharma, who teaches in the Faculty of Law, spoke to me confidentially about the training given to his two daughters by their mother. His wife Shireen is an ex-model, a former beauty queen who married beneath her status, since she hailed from the upper class, something she never let him forget, while he came from a middle-class background and was cast in a more traditional mould.

Shireen encouraged their daughters to spend time with boys, to go to parties, to invite boys home. Prem, being a conventional sort of guy, wasn't too happy with this. You know, fathers worry about their daughters getting banged up or losing their virginity, for that can have major consequences in the Indian marriage marketplace. Shireen explained to him that if he really wanted to protect his daughters from being exploited by randy young Indian lads they needed precisely the kind of exposure she was giving them, because along with the experience of mixing with the opposite sex the girls were learning how to handle situations.

I am sure that you are wondering what all this is leading up to. And yes, why am I going around in circles? Did my sister Ruhno lose her virginity, and if so to whom? Well, to tell you this story, I have to start with how my sister met your son. You don't know, do you?

As a junior member of staff, Ruhno was expected not only to take more classes but also to help with the administration and organising of events. That's how universities function here in India. I'm not sure how it is in the West where you come from, Lord Patel, but it certainly is the case here. Ruhno explained to me how once as a junior lecturer she was obliged to take fourteen classes a week; a senior lecturer was required to take ten, a Reader or Assistant Professor took eight, and a fully fledged Professor took only four. As a result of this hierarchy of work allocation, it all fell on her slender shoulders to organise a series of talks to be given by business leaders for the benefit of the MBA students. Her head of department suggested that for the very first talk she choose someone young and dynamic – someone the students could easily relate to – instead of an ageing, about-to-retire senior executive.

And who better to call than your son Amit. Not yet thirty, but already Executive Director of Patel Properties and Holdings, which in the space of three years had multiplied its asset value from a couple of hundred million dollars to nearly a billion dollars. But the question in Ruhno's mind, as she shared her thoughts with me at the dinner table, was whether he would come. She had persuaded the office secretary to put your son, Amit Patel, directly on the line; they had spoken briefly, and he had agreed to give a small talk. But who knew, with someone as busy and important as your son?

On the big day, true to his word, your son arrived in the college. He brought with him Sunil Gupta, his financial adviser, a tall, completely bald man with mean, beady eyes, about whom I will have more to say a bit later. When Ruhno mentioned his name to me later at dinner, it didn't register at all. There are so many Sunil Guptas in the country, you see. It's like John Smith in the UK.

Amit gave a short, polished talk about the Patel Group, the content of which was recounted to me at dinner that evening by my sister, and I suspect it was modelled on some of the talks that he had heard you give at different prestigious gatherings and universities around the world – including Harvard, I believe, of which you are an alumnus. The class was mostly composed of young, bright, ambitious twenty-year-olds, to whom Amit didn't seem much older, and they lapped up all his words and gave him a resounding ovation. There was a second, louder round of applause when Amit announced that Patel Properties and Holdings would be recruiting five of the brightest students from the Delhi School of Management and starting them off on a six-figure salary.

Ruhno had taken charge of Amit and his friend Sunil upon their arrival, given them a tour of the school's buildings, shown them the lecture halls, the library and the IT centre, offered them refreshments and taken care of them until the time that the Laljani Memorial Lecture – the name the Faculty had dreamed up for this particular talk – was to begin. She told me later that evening that they both seemed very down-to-earth, and they for their part, I am sure, were flattered and their vanity tickled that someone so attractive, educated and sophisticated should be their escort on this occasion. You see, Lord Patel, Ruhno had such a presence that she would light up a room or a gathering simply by being there.

As I explained to you a little earlier, I have no doubt in my mind that back in St Bede's College, Shimla, and then later at the Delhi University School of Management, Ruhno could have had her pick of boys had she just fluttered her eyelashes once. . But she, my darling Ruhno, was either just blissfully unaware of all the attention she naturally attracted, or simply not interested in the various potential possibilities for marriage. You remember I mentioned to you how I had pondered whether her decision to study for a PhD at St Bede's had been prompted by a love affair. To be honest, I wouldn't have been in the least upset if she had been in love with someone, just so long as the boy was a decent sort and from a reasonably well-to-do family, or, even if the last bit had been missing, just so long as I saw some potential in him to become something, even a failed lawyer such as myself. .

I digress again. What I really wanted to tell you was that I am not a very possessive sort of brother, who because he is unmarried would want his younger sister to live with him all her life. In our society, for any girl who has reached her twenties, it's good if she finds a suitable young man to settle down and start a family with sooner rather than later.

Not only did your son Amit make his sudden announcement about recruiting five of the most promising students that day during the high tea that followed the event, which was an affair meant exclusively for the Faculty and the honoured guests; he also mentioned casually to the Dean that he wondered if the Faculty would like to run short financial management courses for some of his junior staff. This, of course, was precisely what the Dean was hoping to hear, so he promptly roped Ruhno into the project, and she was only too pleased to be of help, such was her nature. And so the four of them – the Dean, Ruhno, Amit and Sunil – went off for an after-dinner dessert (for Amit insisted that it was not high tea but a veritable dinner that they had consumed earlier) to the coffee shop at the Oberoi Intercontinental Hotel. During the course of the dessert, the Dean suddenly remembered that some relatives were due to visit him at his residence and begged to leave, assuring Amit and Sunil that he would be available any time they wished to discuss the issue further.

And so Amit, Sunil and Ruhno chatted a bit. Amit confessed that Ruhno had made a big impression on him, and asked Sunil if he didn't think that someone like her would be a valuable asset to the company. Sunil, quick to take the hint, immediately agreed that someone like Ruhno was needed desperately to put all the accountancy procedures in the company beyond any objection from government auditors. Amit then probed whether Ruhno was interested in working for Patel Properties and Holdings at a much higher salary than she was presently drawing. Ruhno, of course, as I've already told you, wasn't at all interested in working for a corporate set-up, and politely but firmly declined. Not one to give up easily, Amit then suggested that she continue to work at the university – they wouldn't dream of stealing her from the students to whom she was so dedicated – but surely the Faculty would have no objection if she did some consultancy work for them. To this Ruhno responded by saying that she would sound out the Dean about their proposal on the next possible occasion. She knew that the Faculty didn't have any objections; rather, staff were encouraged to undertake private consultancy work, so long as it didn't interfere with their Faculty duties, for this helped them to get a real grip on the world of business and not be mere theoreticians. But she didn't want to sound too eager, and in fact wasn't too eager.

After all this business talk, Ruhno explained that she had better be going home, since she needed to prepare dinner for me, her brother, who would be waiting for her and getting anxious. You see, we had our evening meals together most of the time, Ruhno and I. Sometimes I had an urgent case to prepare, and was late coming to the dinner table, but Ruhno always waited for me. Amit then offered to drop her off at our home, explaining that he was going in the same direction. On the way, of course, they began talking of this and that, music, movies, other non-business stuff, and then cutting through the small talk he asked her if she would have dinner with him at the Bali High, a famous multi-cuisine restaurant at the Taj Palace Hotel, the following Sunday.

When Ruhno entered the house that evening, I noticed that her natural radiance was enhanced by a different kind of glow. Her eyes, always shining, were sparkling more brightly than ever and her cheeks bore a faint flush of pink. Oh yes, I could spot the signs easily enough, Lord Patel, for I had never seen her looking like this. After dinner, at which she didn't join me on this occasion, having already eaten, she continued to fuss as usual, but during dessert she casually mentioned the evening's events and what had caused her to be late. She demurely lowered her eyes when she mentioned that Amit had given her a lift home and invited her to have dinner with him on the coming Sunday.

You are curious about my reaction. Of course, I was pleased. The thing is, Lord Patel, that all of us have our natural prejudices, and I must confess that on the basis of your background, which as you know I was familiar with, I automatically assumed that your son was a decent sort of boy. I also trusted Ruhno's judgement to some extent, assuming her lack of interest in members of the opposite sex hitherto was a kind of innate wisdom – yet another addition to the many lovely and special qualities she possessed. It is of course true that your son was running a multimillion-pound business, but to tell you the truth all I wanted for Ruhno was a husband whom she would love and who on his part would love, admire and respect her for the many qualities of her heart, mind and soul, not to mention her stunning good looks.

I could see that Ruhno was waiting anxiously for my reaction, and had prepared *kheer* for the evening's dessert with rather special attention to soften up this crusty old bachelor's heart. I appreciated the rice pudding and asked what she had done to make it so wonderful. She explained that she had cooked it on the small charcoal stove that she had brought over from Shimla. Anyhow, I could see that my compliment had pleased her, but she was waiting for a go-ahead signal from me. In retrospect, that was the moment when I should have told her to forget about having dinner with someone so filthy rich, and possibly she would have listened to me, but at that stage, Lord Patel, I didn't have any reason to suspect that there was anything wrong with Amit. I thought he would be like you. Of course I didn't know you, but I knew you were a man who had created his own future, pulled himself up, a self-made man. So, in that very special way of communication that only very close siblings share, I nodded assent and couldn't help but notice the huge expression of relief that swept across her lovely face.

Were we only brother and sister? I don't think so. We were also in a sense father and daughter, because of the age gap between us. And we were also friends. I, of course, couldn't share what happened in court with her – it would have been too much of a shock for the poor girl's naïve idea about how this terrible world functions – but she did share all or most things with me.

You've heard the poem – a cautionary tale – that begins '"Will you walk into my parlour?" said the Spider to the Fly', haven't you, Lord Patel? Only, in Ruhno's case, unlike the Fly she was too trusting right from the start. At the time, I hadn't even realised that this was happening.

7

I'm glad I persuaded you to try a *fain*, but from the expression on your face I see that you do not like it very much. You feel I have overestimated its value in comparison to a fresh croissant, which a French artist once spoke of as being something to die for. Possibly. You are not a fan of *fains*, we may conclude, but do try a *mathi*, Lord Patel. They go very well with tea. Yes, just have a bite. Only as much as you like. You do like it, I see. Well, then, have another one. I see that you are surprised the *mathis* here are so good. A little later I will show you the place that makes and sells them.

Well, as I was saying, Ruhno and your son Amit began to see each other quite often, so one day when she suggested that I go and meet Amit at his house I didn't think it was a bad idea. In the Indian tradition, it is common for the girl's family to visit the boy's, but in our case, of course, with the death of my parents, there was only poor old me left to represent Ruhno. And so I thought it was all right for me to go and meet Amit in his home, even though you and your wife were not there, especially since I could see that she was very keen for me to meet him and approve her choice.

I got my old grey Fiat (which a grateful client had given me in lieu of fees) washed and serviced, and on a Sunday afternoon we set off for the residence known as the White House in Golf Links.

There were a couple of hulking sentries outside the house. They stared into the car, and then they recognised Ruhno, salaamed and opened the gates that led to the white bungalow. The way they acknowledged first Ruhno's presence and then mine implied to me that my dear little sister had been a rather more frequent visitor to this house than she had led me to believe. No matter, I told myself, this is only to be expected with a girl who's in love.

I had hardly travelled fifteen yards down the driveway when we came to a second gate. A tall, broad-shouldered guard with a black moustache twirled up in the Rajput style approached the car, ostensibly to inspect it, but when he saw Ruhno he seemed to change his mind, for he smiled and greeted her politely.

'This is my brother,' said Ruhno, introducing me to the security guard, and turning to me she added, 'This is Umed Singh, the senior-most guard in this building.'

'Are you from Rajasthan?' I asked Umed Singh, wanting to verify whether my assumption based on his moustache that he was a Rajput was correct.

'*Ji Janab*,' he replied. 'Yes, sir, I am a Rajput.' And as he confirmed his regional identity he gave his moustache a twirl with his fingers.

Then he waved us through the second gate.

We parked next to a shining new Mercedes, one of several luxury cars that were at your son's disposal, befitting his status as the heir apparent to one of the world's biggest industrial empires. We got out of my Fiat and walked across to the main entrance to the house. A liveried doorman let us inside, after pressing a bell, and an attractive thirty-something blonde woman came to meet us.

She was called Maya Richards and introduced herself as Amit's personal secretary. The question I asked myself was what a personal secretary was doing in her boss's house at a weekend. Speaking to us in a clipped British accent, she mentioned that before her present job she had worked at the Burj Al Arab, the internationally renowned seven-star hotel in Dubai. Prior to that, she had studied housekeeping at a reputable school in London, she explained, as she led us along a carpeted corridor, and Amit had asked her just for this weekend to organise the working of the kitchen, the laundry and the garden: this was partly in our honour, and partly because there were plans to hold many official functions and parties at his residence, and he needed just that little bit of expert intervention from her to make things work better. Maya Richards was a classy, smart lady and her general get-up and demeanour led both of us to conclude – we discussed this in soft whispers in Hindi as she moved us along – that she must be fabulously well paid to have left her previous job in such a prestigious hotel just to work for Amit. Ruhno had met her earlier, but they had had little opportunity to talk.

Yet there was something that troubled me about Maya even in that brief encounter. You see, Lord Patel, I've spent so many years in the Thirty Thousand Courts, where I've met so many different kinds of people, that I reckon I'm a pretty good judge of character, and also of signals that people send out all the time. Now Maya was perfectly courteous as far as I was concerned, but I thought I detected a hint of a sneering tone when she spoke with Ruhno. It was as if she were saying, without actually saying: 'Now don't get yourself any airs, darling, just because a handsome young billionaire is giving you some attention.' A small red light began to flash in my brain. I ignored it, told myself that I had perhaps spent too much time in the Thirty Thousand Courts, and needed to be less suspicious and more trusting of people. I told myself I must keep an open mind and, as a court of law was supposed to, give people the benefit of doubt.

Frankly, I was very disappointed when I met your son Amit that first time. He said nothing to me that was out of the ordinary, you see. I have a theory about people, Lord Patel. According to this theory, your true worth as a person has little to do with the amount of success you achieve in your life. There was a time, some years ago, when I represented a couple of Bombay film stars in a criminal case before a magistrate in the Thirty Thousand Courts. They were youngsters who had got drunk in a five-star hotel and had started beating up the bartender for refusing to give them more whisky. When I met them off screen, I was surprised to discover how ordinary and lacklustre they appeared. Not only in terms of personality, you see, but also in what they thought and how they expressed themselves. One of them played a villain on the big screen, and in the film he appeared so charismatic, so magnetic, so impressive and so, dare I say it, intelligent. These were all tricks played by the camera, I then realised. The words spoken on the screen were also not theirs, but scripted by someone more intelligent but with far less status.

I've also met and spoken with a few Supreme Court justices during some of our Bar Association functions that they have consented to attend, and all of them have struck me as petty, bureaucratic and full of prejudices – the worst quality of any for a judge. They do not have – what is the right expression? – the objective, impartial mind. Yet they are Supreme Court justices. In contrast, I have a friend, Ravi Kant, who studied law with me at university. Not only was he a brilliant student, but he had that impartial, objective, unbiased mind that I speak of. Yet he joined as a lowly sub-judge in the Thirty Thousand Courts. A sub-judge! Can you imagine? It sounds like something even less than a real judge – as if it referred to someone undergoing training, waiting to become a real judge. Only three years ago, after many years at this lowest level, he was finally promoted to the rank of a matrimonial judge. This fellow, believe me, is worth ten of your present sitting Supreme Court judges.

What is my point? These days everything is measured in terms of money, is it not, Lord Patel? Money is the measure, even of the man, or rather especially of the man. I saw an American cartoon last week in one of the Sunday papers. Leroy, I think it was called. Just one box in which Leroy's wife is telling him: 'If you are so intelligent, how come you aren't making more money?' And the subtext behind everything your son said that day was the same. If I was so intelligent, as my sister claimed, how come I wasn't making more money?

I cannot be sure what exactly Ruhno had told him about me: possibly that I was a lawyer, brilliant, but not making too much money. When he learnt that I practised law in the Thirty Thousand Courts, he threw back his head in astounded disbelief and gave a huge belly laugh.

And then he said, 'Come now, don't tell me you're serious, how can you possibly be working in that disgusting place? I've been there only once – I had to appear before a court for some minor violation of the Companies Act, not filing the return on time or something – and I made my lawyers, Singhania and Kapoor, promise that they would never ever make me come to the Tis Hazari Courts again. My God, even the bloody fans don't work in that place.'

He turned to Ruhno for sympathy, which she provided, to my consternation, and then spoke highly of his lawyers. 'You know, I have to say that my lawyers are bloody good. They sent two of their brightest young associates to handle the case for me. One of them from the National Law School in Bangalore – the best law college in India, am I right? – and the other one from Yale Law School – can you imagine?' He slapped his thigh. 'Hey, that gives me an idea. Why don't you become an associate of Singhania and Kapoor?'

Mistaking the lack of enthusiasm that I showed for his suggestion for an indication of disbelief on my part at the possibility that they, his snooty lawyers with their fancy office in Connaught Place, would agree to be associated with me, he said, 'We give them a lot of business. They would not be able to refuse me if I put up your name.' My continued silence made him realise I was not interested, and, annoyed at my not behaving like a supplicant, he turned to Ruhno with a look of irritation, as if to say, *Aren't I being nice to your brother, and look at how stupid he is being!*

Inwardly I was furious at his lack of subtlety, at what I considered to be crassness; angry too with my sister for being so passive towards what was certainly an affront on her brother's dignity. But I was wrong about her ignorance of my state of mind, for at this juncture Ruhno deftly turned the conversation towards a newly released Bollywood film starring Shah Rukh Khan, the Bollywood megastar.

I stared out of the window, half listening to the conversation. Even in physical terms I saw that your son wasn't very impressive. You are his father, so I don't want to offend you, but clearly he didn't inherit any of the great good looks that you yourself possessed in your youth. I've seen pictures of you in your younger days – there are a couple on your company's website. Your son was no taller than my sister, certainly a short man by Indian standards. I noted how his hair had been skilfully coiffured at a beauty salon; someone like me, from the old school, doesn't think much of a young man who gets his hair professionally styled. Look, I'll be fair. Despite that small frame your son did radiate a kind of power, a strength of personality, but to me overall it smacked more of arrogance than real leadership.

Small size, short stature – what does any of this matter? I'm not so petty, Lord Patel. None of this would have mattered to me, I tell you, had I been able to like and respect him as a person. I couldn't. I simply didn't like what I saw – and couldn't fathom what my sister saw in him.

Just then I saw a red BMW approaching. The face behind the driving wheel was vaguely familiar, but the car had just entered the driveway and was too far away for me to be certain if it was the person I thought it was.

A maid then walked in to announce that dinner was ready. We moved towards the dinner table, talking all the while. At this moment, the front doorbell rang.

'That must be Sunil,' said Amit, 'my good friend and also the person who fixes my taxes. I've invited him to join us.'

And with these words Amit walked to the door to let his friend and General Manager of Finance into the house. As soon as I saw him, my worst fears were confirmed.

I had spent enough time with criminals, tricksters, frauds, touts, what have you, to be able to identity potential criminality in a person. Amit's glib manner had been so reminiscent of a young criminal on the make that fear had entered my heart as to the future of my young sister. If I had any doubts at all about my suspicions, they were removed as soon as I glimpsed the large, bulky figure of Sunil Gupta.

For I had seen Sunil Gupta inside a courtroom at the Thirty Thousand Courts not long ago: not as a common criminal but, in terms of morality, something far worse. At the time he used to be the Finance Director of Dhoom Television, a popular entertainment channel.

The small red light that had begun to flicker a warning in my brain after meeting Amit's personal secretary, and which I had managed to suppress, now started flashing more intensely and more insistently than before.

Just then, Maya Richards emerged from the kitchen and greeted Sunil like a long-lost friend, with the typical falseness of the over-sophisticated. He pecked her on the cheek and hugged her, having acquired these common western modes of greeting on account of the long years he had spent in the entertainment industry. He held her, I thought, just a few seconds longer than was ordinarily warranted. My suspicions were aroused. I did consider briefly if I was being too much the lawyer, replayed those few seconds of intimacy that I had watched in my mind, and decided, no, I was not overreacting.

The rest of the dinner passed in a kind of blur: lots of small talk, about movies, music, the state of the Indian economy. Sunil and I were perfectly courteous to each other: he on account of being an employee of your son, and I on account of the fact that my beautiful, talented but naïve sister had fallen in love with your son, despite all his failings in courteous behaviour to me, and the implied insults he threw at me that day.

You say that you are embarrassed at your son's behaviour and wish to apologise to me on his behalf? It is not needed, Lord Patel. It is not needed.

* * *

What you may not know, Lord Patel, is that I had handled Sunil Gupta's wife's divorce for her.

Sunil's wife had told me that she couldn't live with him because he was a sex addict.

'And what's wrong with that?'

'Nothing wrong,' she said, 'and I never refused my body to him in all these years. But his addiction doesn't stop with me. He's been having sex with his secretary – I can tell from the tone of his voice when he has been with her – as well as seducing some young women who want to break into the television industry. I tolerated, even accepted all that. But then he joined a circle of top businessmen, who swap their wives, and they teased him for being so dull and conventional. So he wanted me to sleep with some of his friends, and he would get the opportunity to sleep with their wives.'

I had thought that with all these years in the courts I was virtually unshockable, but what she said did shock me. I knew India was changing, but even I had no idea that things were moving so fast. But then, though I had hobnobbed with some of the elite during evenings spent at the Delhi Sports Club, I hadn't moved in quite those circles. Possibly because I didn't qualify. I didn't have a wife to swap.

'I understand,' I said, 'but how do they do the swap?'

'Well,' she said, 'he took me to one of these parties in a three-star hotel in Karol Bagh, where he and his friends had booked several rooms. After dinner and drinks, they all put their car keys into one big bag and shook them up. The men then put in their hands one by one, without looking, and, whichever car keys came up, the owner's wife would be your partner for the night.'

'And that's the reason why your fights began and your marriage broke up?' I said, finding it difficult to conceal my astonishment.

'No other,' she said, with disgust.

Under Indian law, given the context of their matrimonial differences, Sunil had no hope of obtaining a divorce unless his wife consented. And this is where he had to make it worthwhile for her.

Sunil sent me feelers through one of his lawyers. Were I to accept only a moderate settlement for his wife, he could provide me with a substantial kickback: a briefcase stuffed with banknotes, no receipt necessary. But I've always had honest dealings with my clients. In this particular case the judge was known to me from university days but that by itself didn't matter; he was an enlightened, forward-looking man, and should by rights have been sitting in the High Court or Supreme Court.

In consideration of the wife granting Sunil a divorce, I managed to get her a three-bedroom property with a large garden in upmarket South Delhi. Five million rupees in the bank. Quite an achievement, don't you think, Lord Patel. Given the state of India's matrimonial laws, it was a settlement she could not have even dreamed of getting.

Sunil recognised that, and I could see from the gleam in his beady eyes, the last time we met in court, that he hated me. I understood too that he longed to take revenge on me, but he didn't quite know how to achieve that.

Part Four

8

During the days immediately following Ruhno's death, I hardly slept, and fitfully whenever I did. I had macabre dreams in which Lord Patel and sometimes his son Amit figured. When I woke, in a matter of seconds the memory of what had happened would rush in, my body temperature would rise and my mind would experience a strange burning sensation. While I would carry on with my normal duties at the courts, that burning sensation was a kind of anger, a rage even, that stayed with me constantly and accompanied me in all my tasks.

In her last minutes of consciousness with me, Ruhno had named Sunil Gupta as the man responsible for her death. Amit Patel's role in the event that brought about her death remained unclear. When I asked her about Amit, she was unable to speak.

In any event, Sunil Gupta shouldn't be allowed to live much longer, I determined. How to kill him? With my bare hands. I would have loved to do so, but in hand-to-hand combat I knew I was no match. His degenerate lifestyle – the drinking, the womanising, the spousal abuse – had corroded his natural fitness and given him a paunch, but he was still bigger, taller and stronger than me. He was also ten years younger.

And then I remembered someone who could help. Khargosh, the Rabbit. Khargosh was my man.

* * *

There was a criminal case that had come my way because of Ruhno's teaching activities, and that was how I eventually met the man called Suresh, a.k.a. Khargosh, who now became crucial to my carrying out an important act of justice.

Word had spread around the Faculty of Commerce that Ruhno's brother was a lawyer, and so some of my sister's colleagues became my clients. Others came to me through referral. On one occasion I had gone to the Faculty to pick up Ruhno on my way back from work and I was wearing the lawyer's coat and tails. A student in her class, a bright boy called Kalyan, spotted me and approached her after class the next day, asking if I could represent his brother in a criminal case. Ruhno spoke with me in the evening, and then sent the boy to see me at my chambers at an appointed time the following day.

Kalyan came to see me as arranged, very polite and respectful. I was not only going to represent his brother, but was his teacher's brother after all. It turned out that Kalyan lived with his brother and his uncle's family – his parents both having died some years earlier – in a Jhuggi Jhopadi colony in North Delhi. I knew the area. It was a large, sprawling settlement, and though it was referred to as a colony, and the houses were not tin shacks but made of bricks and mortar, it was really just a shallow rung above a slum.

'It's my brother, sir-ji.' He was frail looking, with glasses as thick as the cottage cheese pakoras I insisted he share with me. 'He had a fight with someone.'

'A fist fight?'

'No,' he said, with a guilty expression as if he was the one in trouble. 'He stabbed the man, who is now in hospital. It was a local bully, sir-ji, a *dada* who picked on Suresh. He only acted in self-defence.'

'Have you brought a copy of the FIR?'

'Yes, sir.' He handed me a sheet of paper, a carbon copy with the report inked in blue.

The FIR, short for First Information Report, is an account of an incident prepared by the police. It's not easy to read for someone who hasn't had practice because the Hindi handwriting is fairly illegible, but over the years I had learnt to decipher it.

I skimmed through the report rapidly.

It confirmed Kalyan's story that a big tough neighbourhood bully, a *dada* or gang leader of sorts, had been the one to start the fight. But it spoke of his brother Suresh, too, being a hooligan.

'My brother's been arrested, sir-ji,' Kalyan said, 'and he's still in jail.'

'So tell me the reason for the fight.' I leaned back against my chair, and prepared to listen.

'We have just a single hand pump providing water for bathing and drinking in our section of the Jhuggi, sir-ji. Suresh was having a bath at the pump when Sarla Behn – a cantankerous woman, sir-ji, always fighting with everyone – came to the pump to fill up her bucket. She wanted Suresh to interrupt his bath and move to the side as she was in a hurry to fill her bucket with water. He was lathered with soap and refused. He asked her to wait for a few minutes. An angry exchange of words, sir-ji. She went back and fetched her husband. This fellow is the neighbourhood *dada*. The husband asked Suresh to leave at once, and, when he refused to do so, pushed him. He was a big hefty man, and he set upon Suresh . . .'

Kalyan stopped to nibble nervously at a pakora.

'Keep talking,' I said. 'You haven't done anything wrong. Don't be nervous.'

'Suresh happened to have a knife with him and he used it to defend himself against the bully.'

Happened to have a knife with him. I tossed the 'happened to' around in my mind, trying to think what a judge would make of it.

It was a straightforward enough story on the whole, although Kalyan couldn't explain, when I pressed him, why Suresh had carried a knife with him to the hand pump.

'Is Suresh your older or younger brother?' I dipped a yellow pakora in some green chutney.

'Older by two years, sir-ji.'

'Does he study?'

'He's enrolled in a BA Pass course at Dharam Singh College,' he said brightly.

This was a clear indication to me that Suresh was a laggard in his studies, for despite being two years older than Kalyan he was studying an undergraduate course in a college known for rowdiness. On the other hand, the well-mannered lad who sat in front of me was doing a postgraduate MBA from the prestigious institute where my sister taught.

'Still with the BA? And Dharam Singh?' I bit into the pakora.

'It's true, sir-ji, he is very much behind in his studies.' Kalyan nodded his head sorrowfully. 'And also true that he is a bit hot-tempered. But he's basically a very good person. Exams are just around the corner, next week.' He shot me a pleading look. 'He will lose another year in college if he doesn't get bail.'

'I'll see what we can do,' I said. 'Don't worry. And finish these pakoras before you go.'

I'm always conscientious about the cases I take up, but I gave this matter some special attention. Perhaps it was because it came through a student studying under my sister and I wanted everyone to think well of her, perhaps it was because I sympathised with the struggles of students, or perhaps it was because it was a case of a small man pitted against the village or slum bully, in a manner of speaking. The trial court judge, a short fat man with a moustache as thick as a shaving brush, issued notice to the State, which in this case meant the Police Commissioner for North Delhi, but didn't give us the urgent relief we were seeking.

Normally, I would have told my client, 'Sorry, bad luck, and if you want to appeal I can give you the addresses of some High Court lawyers'; but in this case I decided to go to the High Court myself. I have filed appeals in the High Court on and off, and even before the Supreme Court – if you are an advocate in India you have the right to practise before any court in the land – but generally I just refer cases to colleagues practising there. It interferes too much with my regular practice at the Thirty Thousand Courts for me to be tied up with a case at a superior court, but in this case I personally filed and argued an appeal before the High Court.

The High Court accepted my petition and granted bail, upon my arguing that it was the injured man who had been the aggressor, and that the boy had his exams coming up and would lose a year if he remained incarcerated. I had to argue for a while, since during the course of oral arguments the judge – alternately sharp, alternately indulgent with me, and so also with the prosecutor who was vehemently opposing my request for bail, as if he couldn't quite make up his mind whom to support – played upon the theme that my client was armed with a knife at the time when he was attacked: surely, he argued, this meant that it was not a spontaneous act of violence. But to the prosecution he spoke of how boys can be hot-headed in their youth, and if the boy lost a year he would probably leave his college education and turn wayward. In the end, therefore, he gave in to the prayer in my petition that my client be released on furnishing bail in the sum of 15,000 rupees.

My client had been produced in court at the time of these oral arguments, and I saw him for the first time. He was of medium height, lean but with a muscular build, dark-complexioned, with spiky hair that reminded me of Shakespeare's reference in *Hamlet* to hair standing on end 'like quills upon the fretful porpentine'. He did look a bit like a porcupine, but I guessed that this was the natural condition of his hair, and not the result of any salon treatment. Did I tell you that I had visited the UK during my college days to take part in an international Moot Court competition to represent students at the Law Faculty, with tickets and all expenses covered. In your country I had spotted some youngsters with similar spiky hair, often coloured yellow or pink, but this was not so stylishly done. He also had very long ears that made him look like a rabbit. A cross between a porcupine and a rabbit, I thought to myself. For all his physical distinctiveness, he stood in the corner quietly, like a demure, shy bride. Too demure and too shy to be for real, I thought.

The next day he came to see me at my chambers, a distinct swagger in his walk, and grinning from ear to ear. He was perfectly courteous, but I could see at a glance that here was a lad who had gone the wrong way, and would not easily return to the straight and narrow.

Anyhow, he thanked me profusely, and to show that he meant it he had come with some extra 'fees' for me, which he insisted I take. I took the money, of course – as the saying in the courts goes, if the horse will become friends with the grass, what will he eat? He recounted with pleasure how the Station House Officer who had arrested him had turned purple with rage upon receiving orders from the High Court that he be released.

'You really screwed them in court, *Guruji*,' he said. 'I'd like you to represent me in the court case going on against me.'Although Suresh was now out on bail, as a result of my efforts, the main case against him of stabbing someone would continue.

'What charges have they pressed?'

'So far they've slapped causing grievous bodily harm on me, but that brainless thug I knifed is still in hospital. Some of my friends who casually walked across to the ward to see how he was doing have told me that he might not make it alive. In that case, they will convert the charges against me from causing grievous bodily harm to culpable homicide – possibly even murder.'

'That's bad.'

'Yes, *Guruji*.' He used the respectful title repeatedly while addressing me. 'I need someone like you to defend me in court, and so please, *Guruji* — will you agree to represent me?

I declined politely, explaining that I now did mostly civil cases.

While I would describe myself as more of a civil lawyer than a criminal lawyer, prior to Ruhno's return from Shimla about twenty-five per cent of my practice – most of it referred by Bihari – dealt with criminal cases, mostly minor offences but the occasional rape or murder trial as well.

When Ruhno came home, I deliberately reduced my criminal practice. There was a very good reason for this. In the small apartment we lived in near Delhi University there was no space for an office. I did have an office there while Ruhno was studying in Shimla, but now that she was back and was grown-up we couldn't very well be sleeping in the same room. So there was less space. If you have a criminal practice you will have the odd criminal turning up at your residence, and although many of them are respectful, especially to ladies who carry themselves with poise, grace and dignity – as was the case with Ruhno – you have also the rapist, the child molester or the plain old crook who likes to take advantage of women. And I didn't want to risk any of these types turning up at my home while I was busy arguing matters in the Thirty Thousand Courts. We had friendly neighbours as well as a couple of relatives close by who could be called upon in distress, but I wanted to pre-empt any such situation from arising.

Suresh was in fact precisely the kind of criminal I did not want to represent, even though I knew he would always be respectful to me and to Ruhno were he ever to come to our home. He was, after all, a criminal with the semblance of an education.

He wasn't fazed at all by my refusal. It almost seemed as if he had been expecting it. He excused himself but asked if he could come to consult me with regard to his case. He'd paid me well, so I felt obliged to say that yes, while I wouldn't represent him in the trial court, I was willing to give him advice.

A couple of months later he turned up unannounced one day. The person he had attacked with a knife had died in hospital and, just as he had feared, the police had converted the charges from causing grievous bodily harm to murder. They had not yet cancelled his bail, but Suresh was visibly worried. There had been an eyewitness to the fight between Suresh and the slum gang leader, who had testified in court the same day that Suresh had repeatedly pushed the knife into the man, even when the victim was lying prostrate on the ground. What was he to do?

I explained to Suresh that he was in a bit of a spot, and with this kind of testimony he had better get himself one of the best lawyers in the market. I again told him that I would not represent him but gave him some names of the guys who had a reputation for gruelling cross-examination.

'Your only hope is to get this fellow to contradict himself in court,' I informed him. And then in my teaching style – for I have myself taught at university for a few years alongside my law practice – I explained that under the Anglo-Saxon system of jurisprudence cross-examination is regarded as the greatest engine developed by man to discover the truth. In fact, I told him, if there was no cross-examination of a witness, under the rules of evidence, the main testimony could also not be considered by the judge while deliberating upon a verdict.

He gave a kind of start when he heard me explain the virtues of cross-examination, and then, thanking me profusely for my advice, he wished to press upon me yet more money for giving him my time, and for such invaluable advice, respected *Guruji* – he added the 'respected' now as a small extra flourish. This time I refused to take the money.

He was back a month later, and I asked him how the cross-examination had gone. He explained that there had been no cross-examination, for the witness who had testified against him had been suffering from some kind of depression, and just a week before the date set for cross-examination he had poured kerosene all over his body and set himself ablaze. He was dead now. He could not be cross-examined. And there was no other witness who was willing to testify. God had sent me to him with such excellent advice and saved him by compelling this person to commit suicide.

'Well,' I said a little suspiciously, 'you've been very lucky this time. Now try to stay out of trouble.' He thanked me again, pressed money on me again, which I refused, and was walking out of my chamber when he suddenly turned around and pushed a visiting card towards me.

I took the card from him and saw that there was no name written on it. Just the figure of a rabbit and what seemed like a mobile phone number below this.

He seemed to have made up his mind to come clean with me and didn't hesitate at all when I asked him what the card was about. 'I've started a new business, *Guruji*,' he said.

'And what's this new business?' I smiled. 'Selling rabbit skin?'

'No, sir,' he smiled back, 'more like skinning people. I have a small gang and we are into contract killing. Excellent services, totally professional and very reasonable terms.'

'Not interested,' I replied, giving up any thought of trying to lecture or shame him away from his chosen path, 'but what the hell does this figure of a rabbit have to do with it?'

'That's my mobile phone below, sir – these days the police have started tapping phones so it's best if no names are mentioned. If you ever want anyone killed, sir – and we will offer the very best service to you, for all you've done for me – just dial the number below and ask to speak with Khargosh. That's my secret name. The Rabbit. Don't use my name while calling and don't use your own.'

I told him that I didn't think I would need his services.

'Keep my card,' he insisted politely. 'You never know, you might change your mind.'

I remember turning the card in my hands and thinking to myself that, unlikely as it seemed, if I ever did need services such as those proposed by the young man I would prefer to give him a chance rather than any of the hot-headed murderers whom I had met with lawyer colleagues or sometimes even represented in the Thirty Thousand Courts. There was something about his general demeanour that impressed me. He was polite, quiet, not loud, and had an air of professionalism.

9

I knew I had made the right decision in not telling the police more about the reasons for Ruhno's death. Up to that moment I hadn't enlightened them or anyone else about the real reasons for her suicide. I hadn't mentioned what she had murmured to me in her dying moments, before she collapsed into my arms.

I didn't lose much time in initiating the process of revenge. It was on the fourth day after her death, the day of the *chautha* as we call it, when a religious ceremony is held in the morning. Ruhno's presence that night was so powerful that I had to pour myself a large shot of whisky to settle my nerves and stop my hands from shaking. After the third drink, I walked across to what had been Ruhno's bedroom, which had now been divested of her possessions – I couldn't bear to look at them – and converted back into my office. I picked up the new silver-coloured mobile phone into which I would later insert a different SIM card purchased in a fictitious person's name – these things are easily possible in India – and pushed a few buttons.

'This is *Guruji* speaking,' I said. 'Can I speak to Khargosh?'

'This is Khargosh, *Guruji*.' I could hear the surprise in his voice; he hadn't expected me ever to call.

'Hello, Khargosh,' I said quietly. 'I want to give you a special assignment. The address where you will find this person is the White House in Golf Links.'

'The resident?'

'No, this is someone who visits there very frequently. How will you know who he is? Well, he is a tall, heavily built man, who wears a wig – the wig is very evidently a wig, if you know what I mean – and he drives a brand-new red BMW. He lives in Jamnapar, across the river, and most days he drives home from the White House after dinner.'

'The payment, *Guruji*.' He spoke softly.

'Not a problem. Come over to my office tomorrow.'

I had decided that if Khargosh refused for some reason, I would carry out Sunil's killing myself. What mattered to me was that he should die, that he should not be allowed to live on this planet any more, and it mattered little whether I personally wrung his neck or had Khargosh make it look like a 'hit-and-run' accident. It would be a bonus if he suffered before dying, and I was determined to witness it.

Khargosh had come up with a different plan from the usual hit-and-run. In this scenario, he said there would be just a single associate with him on that day.

'Are you sure you'll manage with just one person?' I said.

'No problem, *Guruji*. You won't doubt he's enough when you see him.'

And it's true that when I saw him my doubts finally disappeared. A huge hulk, he was built like a wrestler with ripping muscles and a nasty scar running from his right eye all the way down to his neck. A deep cut. I didn't doubt that he alone would be enough for Sunil Gupta.

On the thirteenth day after Ruhno's death, another ceremony, known as the *terveen*, was held. It was attended by all my relatives. Pain lashed me once again. I was glad we had arranged the kill for that day.

It was a Friday, the day that Patel Properties always threw a big bash at the White House. Only a few higher-ups within the organisation were invited, as I had learnt from Ruhno, who herself never attended.

* * *

Khargosh had one of his associates parked outside the White House, and his task was simply to call and let us know when the man driving the red BMW left.

Deep Cut, Khargosh and I were waiting inside a black Ambassador pulled up on the side of the main road that led on to the bridge beneath which the Yamuna flowed. It had been raining heavily for the past few days and the waters of the river were swollen.

It was half past two in the morning when the mobile in Khargosh's pocket buzzed. I saw him listen carefully for a few minutes.

'He's off.' Khargosh smiled, flashing white teeth in the darkness. '*Guruji*, if you can just keep an eye out.'

I was sitting in the rear seat and was best positioned to spot any approaching car. I twisted around and fixed my gaze on the road, fearful that there would be a slip-up, even though I knew it would be at least ten minutes before Sunil Gupta's car would appear in my line of sight.

It was raining, and the white street lights reflected off pools formed on the wet road surface. There was no sign of man or beast. Even the kerosene lamps in the populous slum that lay beside the river had gone out.

And then I saw the BMW.

'He's coming!' I shouted. 'Let's go.'

Khargosh turned the key in the ignition, revved up the engine, and we were racing towards the bridge. We were doing the maximum speed our small round car could do. We knew we would be no match for the red giant hurtling towards us, and so we needed to reach the bridge before he did.

Deep Cut said, 'Let me call Tabrez.' He keyed a number into his mobile, spoke for a few seconds and switched it off.

'All okay,' he announced.

Tabrez was another of Khargosh's associates. He had parked his car behind ours, near the turning. He too was waiting for Sunil's car to appear. As soon as it passed him, he was to drive his vehicle forward and slant it across the road to block the path of any other vehicle coming our way. He'd have to hold up the traffic for just five or ten minutes. We counted on that being enough time to do what we had to.

We had timed our journey in a few trial runs from the point where we were stationed to the point where the bridge began, so I knew it took us six and a half minutes on average. We could see Sunil's car as soon as he turned into the main Ring Road, and I knew by calculating the lead we had over him and dividing it by so many miles per hour that try as he might he wouldn't arrive at the bridge before then.

I looked at my watch, then turned towards the small red dot approaching. It became larger until it was the size of a bride's *bindi*, then a football, and then it was almost upon us.

'Faster!' cried Deep Cut. 'Faster!'

We were at the bridge on schedule with half a minute to spare. The red BMW was closing in.

We stopped right in the middle of the road, so that there was no way for him to get past. A yellow-and-black-striped wall partitioned the two lanes, and Sunil couldn't have made a U-turn even if he had somehow managed to guess what awaited him.

Deep Cut and I remained inside our car, but Khargosh got out, stood on the pavement, and waved at Sunil to stop.

He didn't have a clue. He got out of the car roaring drunk and began to curse.

'You fucking idiot!' he shouted. 'What do you mean by parking your car in the middle? Pull over to the side, *bhenchod.* Does this road belong to your dad?'

Khargosh laughed. A tinkling sound exuding professional calm and poise. It was in harmony with my own inner feelings at that moment, and for all of two seconds I allowed myself to enjoy the sensation of cool air that wafted into the car. Everything was under control. This scumbag had got it coming now.

'If a big man like you could help us push the car,' Khargosh said, 'we'll soon be on our way.'

'What do you need my help for, you fucking moron?' Sunil blustered as he staggered forward and peered into the interior of our car. 'I can see you've got people inside. Can't they help?'

'My friend is sick,' Khargosh said, 'but I can ask if he can help us if you like. *Abbe*, Safdar, can you come out and help?'

'No problem,' rumbled Deep Cut as he opened the door and in one swift move drew his full bulk out. '*Guruji*, why don't you join us?'

I had the pleasure of seeing the panic enter Sunil Gupta's eyes when he saw Deep Cut. His eyes dropped to the fourteen-inch knife that the big man held in his hands. And then realisation gradually dawned when he turned and caught sight of me.

'I'll give you whatever you want.' He quickly removed his watch.

Deep Cut collected it in a perfunctory manner. His scowl didn't disappear.

'*Kameez utar*,' he ordered. 'Take off your shirt.'

'Take what you want,' Sunil pleaded. He pulled out his wallet, pushed open the flap and offered it to Deep Cut.

Deep Cut scowled. 'That's why I'm saying, *bhenchod*, take off your shirt.' He pocketed the wallet.

Sunil started to unbutton his shirt. He shot me a quick glance, as if to assess whether there was any possibility of mercy. And he never looked at me again.

'Trousers now,' Deep Cut said, grabbing the shirt.

'No, please . . .'

'*Bhenchod.* I said trousers.'

Sunil made a lunge at Deep Cut at this point, and almost got him off balance, but the blade entered his stomach and soon he was both squealing and leaking blood like a pig.

He fell down, reddening the pavement, and continued to make pleading gestures. Despite his weakened state, he slowly started to remove his trousers.

I thought of how a few days earlier Ruhno lay naked and defenceless and how she must have looked at him with soft, pleading eyes. And this man, this man now begging for his life, must have grinned, possibly laughed, and then gone ahead and violated her. I watched Sunil's humiliation with cold pleasure.

Sunil paused midway, having unzipped his trousers and pushed them down to his knees. Deep Cut ripped them off in a single pull.

'That's the only thing we won't do, you evil fucking prick. We won't rape you.' Deep Cut stared at him. '*Aao bhai*, Khargosh. This man is stinking so badly I think we need to send him for a bath.'

And with Khargosh catching Sunil by the legs and Deep Cut holding him from the head they heaved and sent the body tumbling over the railing. Down, far down towards the swirling waters the white body streaked. There was a loud splash.

Khargosh picked up the trousers, went through them rapidly and threw them across the railing as well.

'There, that's done.' Deep Cut smiled. 'Let's get going now, brothers.'

And in a few seconds we were off.

For some reason a line from *Julius Caesar* kept coming to my mind as I thought of that fat naked body hurtling towards the waters of the Yamuna.

O! what a fall was there, my countrymen.

Singularly inappropriate, but it made me laugh. I felt light, almost giddy. It would perhaps be an exaggeration to say that I rejoiced, but I had the feeling that I was floating like a cloud bathed in moonlight.

'*Abbe, bottle khol*,' Deep Cut said.

'Hold on a few more minutes,' Khargosh insisted.

It was not until our car had driven past the pale orange traffic lights at the Income Tax Office junction that Khargosh opened a bottle of Diplomat, a popular brand of whisky. He took a swig and passed the bottle to Deep Cut, who held it to his mouth for a long swallow before passing it on to me. Normally I drink only the premium Indian brands aside from Scotch, but on this occasion I decided to make an exception.

'You guys finish it off,' I said, and returned the bottle. It was foul-tasting stuff.

In the front of the car, the drink soon got to them and the car wasn't on a smooth track any more.

'Why did you get him to take his shirt off?' Khargosh said.

'I liked it. His trousers would have been of no use.'

'Didn't you want his underwear?' Khargosh sniggered. 'It was branded.'

Deep Cut muttered, '*Bhenchod.*'

And then they were giggling like a couple of schoolboys.

They dropped me off on the main road near Mukherjee Nagar.

'See you, *Guruji*,' Khargosh said. 'Satisfied?'

'More than.'

Back in my apartment I opened a bottle of Vat 69. My euphoria didn't last long. Halfway through the bottle I found myself once again in the cold grip of despair. The tentacles of grief closed around me.

I now started to think about Amit's possible role in the whole episode. Had Amit known that Sunil was going to rape Ruhno? The question went round and round in my mind that sleepless night. The more I thought about it, the more it seemed unlikely to me that Sunil Gupta would have risked committing such an act without Amit's knowledge, and perhaps his active agreement. As an employee of Patel Holdings and Properties, even as Amit's best friend, he wouldn't have dared to lay a finger on Ruhno had Amit indicated that she was in any way important to him. But I couldn't be certain of Amit's involvement. Ruhno had said nothing against him, and as the morning dawned I concluded that I would have to give him the benefit of the doubt.

Part Five
Tea-break

10

Well, Lord Patel, I trust that Hetram, my *munshi*, took good care of you while you were waiting in my chambers. You might have been disconcerted at not finding me here when you arrived, but instead someone else, with a slightly odd-shaped head. Not to worry. Hetram may have a rather crazy, deformed, dwarfish look about him, but he is the kindest, nicest man you will find in these precincts.

This is the reason I keep him as my *munshi*. He is a man I can trust, and, believe me, within these corrupted, decrepit structures it is often difficult to find someone like that. Hetram lives in a town called Baghpat, in India's most populous state, Uttar Pradesh, which happens to be a three-and-a-half-hour commute from Delhi. That's about half the time it takes you, Lord Patel, to fly from London to New York, a trip that I imagine you make quite frequently, since you control huge financial interests in the UK as well as in the US, and now even in China and India too. Every morning the poor fellow takes the five o'clock train to make the journey to these courts, and every evening he takes the train back to Baghpat. He travels ticketless, of course, just like so many thousands of other passengers travelling huge distances to the capital where they can find work. I once asked him how he amused himself during the long ride into town. He explained that, in the particular compartment he chose to travel in, it was always easy to find someone to talk to, for these were regular passengers and everyone recognised each other – not like your standoffish British rail commuters who unfurl a copy of the *Guardian*, or the *Telegraph*, as the case may be, and ignore all their fellow passengers. Apart from having people to chat with, he could, he told me, join the group playing *teenpatti* or the group singing *bhajans*. Hetram disapproves of gambling; moreover, his slowness would irritate the other players, and I'm confident he would generally lose, so I'm not surprised he has never joined the gambling group. He has, however, on occasions joined the bhajan choir, and he is a great believer in Mata Vaishno Devi. One of these days, he has sometimes confided in me, the Goddess will solve all his problems.

Apart from the fact that I can trust Hetram, there is one more thing that I like about him. He is generally very cheerful, despite all the difficulties he faces. Sometimes a client will remark to me privately that Hetram looks a bit retarded. But no, I wouldn't say Hetram is retarded – though it's true that he's a bit slow. He is not alert and *chaalu* – the Hindi word for a cleverness that borders on trickery – like many of the court clerks employed by my colleagues. Once I had a doctor who came to me to ask me to represent him in a malpractice suit, and he took one look at Hetram and said he was a Down's child. I've read about children who suffer from Down's syndrome, but they possess, to my mind, more or less some degree of learning disability; and Hetram is slow, as I said, but is certainly not disabled in his capacity to learn. He has one thing in common with children who suffer from Down's syndrome, however. Those children are said to be cheerful in nature – it has always intrigued me how this could be so, for surely these things are not biologically ordained but rather a matter of one's temperament as well as circumstances – but Hetram is certainly cheerful. You need a cheerful face in these surroundings. Every month a litigant loses his mind in the courts over here. He begins shouting at a judge, or starts ranting and raving in public, and then of course the police have to take him away.

Hetram is reticent about his past, but through bits and pieces of information divulged to me over time I have come to understand that he ran away from home when he was a young lad and has been on his own ever since. He has no plans to get married. He doesn't want to discuss the reasons why he left home, and after a couple of failed attempts I have decided not to probe any further. Before he became a *munshi* in the courts, he worked for some years as a sort of pharmacist in an Ayurvedic dispensary. As well as working in the factory, he sold goods across the counter in a shop located near the North Indian religious town of Haridwar. As someone involved with the manufacture and sale of these medicines, he acquired over time a fair amount of knowledge about the usefulness of various Ayurvedic medicinal preparations. He once gave me something for malaria called *giloi*, which worked better than the quinine I had taken earlier for the same problem but did not cause me any weakness; the allopathic quinine makes you so weak that you find it difficult to raise yourself from the bed and walk to the toilet. Another time, I developed a skin rash, something called urticaria, which the allopathic doctors were unable to cure even after several months of treatment. Hetram bought some ingredients with money that I gave him and prepared a yellow paste for me, and after applying it over the places where the rash appeared – this is a moving rash, which travels all over your body every few hours – within two weeks I was cured. Permanently. The rash never returned.

* * *

Ah, the tea has arrived. Good, good. This is Saeed, the tea stall owner who sends tea and *fains* to my chambers, and on request he gets me some *mathis* from another shop a little further down the same road. For most lawyers he sends one of the lads who work for him with the tea, but with me he often comes over himself. We have a special relationship. He is a tall, strapping fellow, isn't he? Looks like a professional wrestler, you say. Well, he has been in lots of fights, I understand! I wouldn't want to get on the wrong side of someone like that – would you?

We are more than three thousand lawyers in this court complex, so we provide employment to at least fifty or sixty illegal stalls that have set up shop on the pavement just outside and provide us with tea and various kind of biscuits that you may now no longer be familiar with. I'm sorry I can't offer you Shrewsbury biscuits! Will another lowly *fain* or *mathi* do? Ah, you are content with just a cup of tea. Nothing else. Very well.

You thought Saeed was looking at you in a funny kind of way, you say – in a sly kind of way. Well, he doesn't generally look at people with such an expression, but if he was looking at you in a 'funny' kind of way, I can make a guess as to why he looked at you like that. But I will explain later.

My *munshi*, Hetram, progressed from being a bricklayer, to working in the Ayurvedic medical store, to being a lawyer's clerk – but Saeed, who brought us our tea a while ago, is an instance of reverse hopping. You see, Lord Patel, you live in such rarefied surroundings, so completely cut off from the hard social realities that others have to face, that it would never occur to you there is a rise and fall in rank and status even within the underclass. Saeed has also worked on construction sites. This is something he has in common with Hetram, about the only thing perhaps, as they are very different kinds of persons and personalities – just as you and I have our legal studies in common (funny, isn't it?) – but instead of becoming a *munshi*, though I grant you the two roles are completely unrelated, he became a contractor. Difficult to believe? Indeed, but it's the truth, for I've seen him myself. He did small building contracts renovating houses, employing some of his erstwhile labourer friends, and then a few years ago he came to the Thirty Thousand Courts and even helped build and modify some of the lawyers' chambers: that was when I first saw him. His construction business started to make losses, however – don't ask me how – and he had debts to pay, so he gave up the idea and has now started this tea stall business, just outside the courts, and has been slowly and steadily paying them off.

He wants to get back to the construction business but needs some capital. About six months ago I promised him a loan, and you'll be interested to know that I gave him the loan not two days ago, and this is the last week he will run this tea stall, for now that he has the capital he will soon be starting again with small construction jobs. I believe he has a couple of offers in hand.

I have told Saeed that the money I have given him is a loan, but that is just to make him cautious and encourage him to work harder and more carefully at his business. In truth, though, the money is a gift. Charity? No, Lord Patel, not charity at all. What Saeed has done for me is beyond repayment.

Let me tell you how we first became friends. You see, Saeed has now been running his tea stall for over two years. About the time when he set up his tea stall, he was looking for lawyers to order tea from him, and my chamber happens to be just across the street from where he has his stall – there are these very small gates that open out into the street, kissing gates I believe you call them – so he was very disappointed when, after a few orders of tea, I would bypass him and order tea from Harish, a tea stall owner who had his small operation another thirty yards away.

Anyhow, one fine day Saeed stormed into my chamber and in an aggressive tone of voice demanded to know why I wasn't ordering tea from his stall but going to Harish's. Now, I generally don't tolerate aggression, especially from the underclass, but in his case I somehow sensed that he liked me and somehow felt hurt that I was not ordering tea from his stall, so I sat him down, in the very chair in which you are sitting, Lord Patel, and explained to him that when I ordered tea I wanted it pronto, in less than three minutes preferably, and the other guy, Harish, who was further away, nevertheless sent me the tea faster than he did. The anger disappeared from his face; he was contrite with apologies and said that he now understood my requirement, and that I should continue to order tea from his stall and henceforth the tea would be sent off within two minutes. Okay, I said, we will order tea from you as well, and I instructed Hetram accordingly.

So over the next few weeks I ordered tea from him as well as from Harish, and then one day he came to me and asked if I was satisfied with the delivery and quality of the tea, and when I said yes, he then suggested that I order tea from him exclusively. I considered his request for only a few seconds but declined, explaining that Harish too had given me good tea and good service and that he, Saeed, must learn to be not greedy but fair-minded. He didn't press the issue, but I could see that I had gone up a notch in his estimation as someone who believed in a kind of justice, even if I practised law at the Thirty Thousand Courts. And over the next few months both Saeed and Harish continued to supply me with tea, biscuits, *fains* and *mathis* – although these *mathis* are not from his shop but a much better place, where I will take you in a short while. Then Harish died – poor fellow was suffering from tuberculosis, he had left it too late, and the drugs didn't work on him – and after that Saeed become my exclusive tea and biscuit supplier.

A word about Saeed's aggression. Yes, he has what you in the West would call an 'anger management problem', and I believe that this was the reason why he was in prison on several occasions. Oh yes, my tea supplier Saeed, the construction worker-turned-contractor-turned-tea-stall-owner, has been in and out of prison several times. Mostly scrapes, fights, that sort of thing. As you have noticed, he is quite well built and muscular – the construction work possibly helped build up his muscles and tone his body generally.

Yes, Hetram? *Nahin*, you don't need to be here any more. Please go and amuse yourself whichever way you like. That's one of the things that make Hetram compatible with me. You see, unlike other lawyers, I don't want a *munshi* who is sitting about in my office all the time. That means I have to think of things for him to do. I would rather just be alone doing nothing in my office. It is for this reason that some of my colleagues believe I'm paying Hetram far too much. But this is the way I like it. For others to be free, just as I myself like to be free.

If you stop to think about it, in a way lawyers are not very different from people like Hetram and Saeed. Of course, our professional code of ethics bars us from doing any other kind of business simultaneously. At the same time, while this is the rule, there are many of us who breach that rule. For example, in this row of chambers, just two doors away in the eastern direction, there is Mr Tomar, a lawyer who also runs a real estate business. Yes, it's true. Well, I guess he is a goldfish in the ocean while you, Lord Patel, are a gigantic blue whale, for you do have a huge real estate empire now, don't you? Mr Tomar charges the normal commission that a real estate agent charges for the sale of properties and, I'm told, explains to his clients from that business how lucky they are to have a lawyer check out everything from the title of the property to the language in the sale deed, at no extra cost.

Now, you might argue that this kind of extra work, though strictly speaking not permitted, is closely related to the kind of work that we lawyers do, and I will grant you that. But then take a look at the side occupation practised by Mr Bhushan, who is just three chambers away in the western direction.

Mr Bhushan comes from a family of priests. They have been the priests in a centuries-old Goddess Durga temple at Kalkaji in South Delhi. Now of course the family has enlarged during this time, and therefore they have divided among themselves the right to be priests in the temple. It is not only a matter of prestige, for if you happen to be the priest you also collect a fair amount of money that is given by the devotees. Bhushan is the eldest son in his family and has been allotted three weeks every year for being a *pujari* or temple priest, so he makes sure that no court case falls during that period – which period incidentally keeps fluctuating every year – and he tells me that, no matter what time of the year it is, the collections are always substantial. Sometimes he is lucky in the draw – yes indeed, they have a draw for the dates to be allotted! – and he gets to sit during the Diwali or Dusshera festival, and then of course the money simply pours in.

* * *

Ah yes, I was telling you how I never had enough 'venture capital' to venture out, so to speak, into the higher echelons of the legal practice. I, who was a gold medallist at the Law Faculty of Delhi University, had to be content with practising in the lowest of the lower courts. The famous, or rather infamous, Thirty Thousand Courts.

It wasn't that I didn't try. Let me tell you a bit about my beginnings at the Bar.

Usually, Lord Patel, in the case of a fresh law graduate who intends to practise law, a relative, a parent or a friend recommends a senior lawyer who is in need of an assistant and with whom he can begin his training. I suppose it's not very different in your country, is it? In India the expression 'senior lawyer' does not denote an elderly lawyer, since there are many aged and infirm lawyers commonly seen at the Sub-Registrar's Office who barely manage to eke out a living. It refers instead to that category of experienced lawyers who have over the years accumulated so many briefs that they need to have the assistance of one or more junior advocates if they are to manage at all.

Twenty-five years ago, when I had just entered the legal profession, the new entrant, commonly referred to as a 'junior', was generally not paid anything for the first six months of his training. I personally know some juniors who were not paid anything for as long as three years. During this period they remained dependent on their parents for financial support and sustenance.

It is a curious paradox that whereas a *munshi* – someone like Hetram – is quite naturally paid a monthly salary, juniors are very often paid nothing. A junior is, however, often obliged to carry out a substantial amount of clerical work and is prevailed upon to do odd jobs and run errands, and therefore some of them refer to themselves as 'bonded labourers'!

After finishing law school I went, as it were, from chambers to chambers in the Supreme Court and the High Court (in the lawyers' chambers complex), introducing myself to senior lawyers and professing my willingness and desire to assist and learn. The catch, however, was always the question of remuneration, my family's situation being such that I needed to bring some money home. I didn't want to be talking about my personal problems to anyone, least of all to lawyers whom I had never seen before in my life, so I raised with them the issue of some minimum remuneration as a matter of right and not one of necessity. What was their response? No dice. Junior lawyers were available free, so why should they pay? One senior lawyer whom I met in the Supreme Court expressed his amazement at what he called my 'style', which was to walk into his office and demand paid employment, and he wished to know how I expected remuneration if I wasn't bringing him any business.

You see, Lord Patel, there were fresh entrants into the profession who came from well-connected families, who were paid handsomely by their seniors almost from the first month mainly because their 'seniors' hoped to derive benefits from the influential connections of their trainees. For instance, Lord Patel, if your son Amit had studied law, just as you and I have, and wished to start a law practice in India, he would have been given a very high starting salary, no questions asked, because of the business he would be certain to bring.

But why be a lawyer? Why not work for a well-paying company, such as your own for instance, as a legal officer? You see, Lord Patel, in those days the Indian private sector had fewer opportunities for qualified lawyers. I tried without any success to become a management trainee in one of the big Marwari companies; they preferred candidates who had studied commerce, economics and management. There was only one assured way for a young lawyer starting out to earn money right from the beginning, and that was if I began my practice at the lowest of the lower courts. And so, Lord Patel, I decided to come to the Thirty Thousand Courts and try to earn some money. Unlike the superior courts, where I would have had to work as a low-paid or unpaid bonded labourer for many years, here I could start to earn something right away. The commercial companies had rejected me because I had no MBA or degree in economics, but by a strange irony I soon began to work in the Sunday 'bazaar'.

The lawyers whom I met in the Supreme Court often raised arguments in court on how it was the duty of the State to work for an egalitarian society, where there was no concentration of wealth, where there was equal opportunity for all in education, work and livelihood, and where there was social justice. These lofty ideals were extolled in open court by senior lawyers who did not reflect for a minute on some of their own duties to their profession, such as trying to help the cash-strapped junior lawyers who assisted them. As the expression goes, charity surely begins at home.

In my own personal case, charity did begin at home. What do I mean? I mean quite simply, sir, that I had responsibilities.

And that reminds me that I have a responsibility towards you, my guest as well. It is now nearing lunchtime. My stomach is protesting. What say we have a short walk across the street outside to Nathu's? I promise you that the food will be simply delicious. Oh, it's not far at all. Do watch your step when you walk out, Lord Patel. You see, my chamber is built at a slight elevation and sometimes people stumble if they are not careful. You've noticed that, have you? Well, what with climate change concerns these days, Lord Patel, you never know, do you? As it is, the monsoon can sometimes be really torrential in Delhi. We at the Thirty Thousand Courts are situated in a relatively low-lying part of Delhi, and when it rains it all becomes muddy and sometimes there can be low-level flooding.

Part Six

11

Two days after Sunil Gupta's body was fished out of the Yamuna, the police came to my residence and arrested me.

I was already alert to the fact that they might suspect me and try to arrest me, so the day after Sunil Gupta's killing I met with Mr Chaudhury, President of the Thirty Thousand Courts, and apprised him of the possibility that I might be arrested. Someone trying to pin a false charge on me, I told him. He didn't ask too much about the details. These things happen off and on. My case was not unique. It was not the first time that a lawyer from the Thirty Thousand Courts would be arrested. Mr Chaudhury just told me to send him an SMS text message from my mobile phone if and when it happened, and he would take care of it.

The police did allow me a quick, unsupervised visit to the toilet when they arrested me, and while I peed I drew out my cellphone, found Mr Chaudhury's name in the address book, quickly texted the words 'Arrested and taken to PS Daryaganj', and pressed the Send button. I knew they wouldn't allow me to make a phone call, especially if they were planning to torture me, as I suspected they were.

In police stations all over the country prisoners are commonly administered what have come to be known as 'third degree' methods by the police, almost as a matter of routine. Third degree, which is nothing but torture plain and simple, has infinite possibilities, depending upon the cruelty and ingenuity of its perpetrators. Thus it is not uncommon to hear horrendous accounts in Indian newspapers of prisoners being hung upside-down and having sticks shoved up their private parts, or being subjected to electric shock treatment. It was fair for me to assume that I would not be exempted, though I did hope, desperately, that, by the time they warmed up, rescue would be at hand.

The Station House Officer at the Daryaganj Police Station had been telephoned by Mr Chaudhury soon after we reached the police station, at the time when I was in an adjacent room and being given the preliminary treatment that consisted of light and sound effects – being made to sit in a room with bright lighting and have policemen growl at me. The SHO tried to explain to the Bar Association President that these were orders from higher-ups, and that he didn't really know what charges I was being arrested on. That was all the confirmation that Chaudhury needed. The Thirty Thousand Courts Bar Association was on strike even before the courts opened that day! And before noon the Law Minister of the country had personally called the Commissioner of Police to demand an explanation of what was happening.

Even though we receive disparaging and contemptuous remarks from those who are forced to come to these 'portals of injustice', and also indeed from our legal brethren in the superior courts, the fact of the matter is that we do carry considerable clout.

The sad-looking constable was still swinging his cane when the Station House Officer rushed inside the room, the torture room, and commanded his minions to stop at once.

'Who authorised you to hit this gentleman?' he roared at them, while they stared back at him nonplussed. 'Don't you know he is a lawyer? Stop all this nonsense at once!'

The police gave up any further attempts to interrogate me. They just said they'd had orders from the Commissioner who had been approached by Amit Patel. I was given tea, cold drinks, samosas, pakoras, and lunch from the famous Peshawari restaurant. It was VIP treatment all the way. In the afternoon five lawyers drove down to the police station to collect me personally. The police didn't resist. Aside from all the pressure that had been put on the police, they recognised one simple fact. We were from the same tribe; not real brothers, but close cousins at any rate.

The police didn't get anything out of me, but I did find out something new and disturbing from them. The Station House Officer who was in charge of Daryaganj Police Station revealed to me that Amit Patel was terrified that I might try to get him killed.

'These rich young kids,' he scoffed, as he put a *paan* into his mouth, 'you know what they are like. Did you threaten him or something?'

I shook my head.

'In that case, did you threaten his friend Sunil Gupta?' he asked. 'You know the person I'm talking about. The papers were full of it last week. The fellow used to work for Amit Patel.'

I admitted that I knew Sunil Gupta, but said that I hadn't threatened him.

slung across his shoulders, and I knew that although he might think twice he would ultimately not hesitate to use it.

He strode up to me and scowled, but before he could open his mouth I stared him down and told him in Hindi, in no uncertain terms, to tell his *madarchod malik* – his 'motherfucking master' – that he wouldn't be safe living inside the White House for very long, and as a matter of fact I'd pull him out of his hiding place, and soon, very soon, before Holi was over, he would be in my custody, and I would decide then what to do with him.

Moving back a step or two, so I had a clearer vision of the White House and anyone inside had a clearer vision of me, I said, in English this time: 'I will drag you out of your hiding place, you fucking coward, and I will kill you! Do you hear me? I will kill you.'

The taxi driver had stepped out of the Ambassador, and he and Umed Singh pushed me back into the car. I didn't resist much. We turned back and started driving towards the main Ring Road. Anguish lacerated me and drew blood. Inside, I was haemorrhaging uncontrollably.

I don't know why I spoke those threatening words, because, as well as sounding like something from the script of the worst Bollywood melodrama, until then I had no plan to kidnap Amit. All I knew was that I wanted to kill him, and as soon as possible. But those strange words came out of my mouth, and then, as things turned out, Amit Patel had to vacate his residence at Golf Links and I was instrumental in making that happen. Was it a premonition, I wonder? If I had had any vestigial doubts concerning Amit Patel's role in Ruhno's death, they disappeared during that visit. Why had Amit banned my entry, if he wasn't nursing a guilty conscience?

12

It was a confidence trickster called Bihari who helped me get Amit Patel removed from the White House in Golf Links. Bihari was someone who had put a lot of work my way during the difficult days when I needed money for my mother's medical treatment.

'Why me?' my brain screamed when we received the report, and then quickly corrected the thought to 'Why us?' I was older and better prepared to bear the loss of my father, and the anxieties caused by my mother's illness, but Ruhno – my poor little sister – was only nine. I hugged her close and wiped her tears.

'Nothing will happen to Ma,' I assured her. 'Don't worry, sister. Nothing will happen.'

The junior doctor I met at the government hospital where we first took my mother told me that she couldn't be cured.

'It's just impossible,' he said.

'Can you explain this to me in terms I can understand?'

'Have you ever seen a bad road accident?'

I nodded. There were frequent accidents at the crossing near the Thirty Thousand Courts and I had witnessed a couple of these.

'Well, then,' he said, 'it's exactly like that. I am a surgeon and I've worked in OPD where they suddenly bring in accident patients whose bodies are too damaged for anything to be done to save them. They are going to die. And the same is the case with your mother's stomach. I have seen the endoscopy report and it tells me in so many words that she cannot be cured.'

The junior doctor's explanation was chilling. It didn't stop me from talking to the most senior doctor in the hospital, who confirmed the diagnosis and the forecast.

'Six months at the most,' he said.

I wasn't about to give up. Ma. We couldn't lose her, Ruhno and I.

But I needed money to be able to explore alternative medical possibilities. And we didn't have any money.

Where was I going to get it from?

* * *

For most first-generation lawyers who do not possess extraordinary social contacts, the building-up of a law practice is a process that takes several years. My decision to practise law at the trial court was the logical fallout of my family's financial situation, since there were at least chances of some bail applications and other miscellaneous work for me there.

With my mother's illness, I needed to increase my earnings. We were still knee-deep in debt owing to money borrowed to pay for the expenses incurred through my father's illness.

Mr Chaudhury, President of the Bar Association a few times, suggested to me, when I spoke to him of my predicament, that I hang around the criminal courts on Sundays, when I would be sure to pick up something from the Court of the Duty Magistrate. There would generally be only a single judge sitting in small district towns, but in a big city like Delhi we had two and sometimes even three Duty Magistrates who presided on Sundays and other holidays. And so I turned up in court as advised. It was an illuminating experience.

* * *

The entire court complex wore a deserted look on Sundays, in sharp contrast to the hustle and bustle of a normal working day. The verandas and open spaces outside the court building's concrete structure resembled a huge second-hand furniture market: endless rows of empty tables, chairs and benches, most of them chained to one another or to pillars to make sure that nobody went off with them. Even junk is valuable in India. These battered and bruised tables and chairs wouldn't even qualify as junk elsewhere, and would have been destroyed years before they ever reached such a state.

On these days only ten to fifteen advocates turned up regularly. They would park themselves near the main entrance to the hall where the Duty Magistrate held court.

An equivalent if not larger number of middlemen or touts hung around. They would hover at the entrance to the court building and rush towards the clients, customers, victims – call them what you will – as soon as they spotted them. The influx of these victims would start around noon and continue until two o'clock, when the magistrate would start hearing the miscellaneous applications.

As soon as an auto rickshaw drove up to the main entrance, the touts would rush towards it and accost the client. The client would generally choose a particular tout, maybe somebody whose face he found more attractive, trustworthy or whatever he was looking for.

After capturing his victim, the tout then dragged him to a particular advocate with whom he had a 'setting' – a pre-set deal – and pretend to be in a hurry. Then in even greater haste papers were pulled out, there was furious scribbling and shuffling of papers, and the victim was told to hand over the money – hurry, hurry!

After the client had paid the fee to the lawyer, the tout would rush back to his post for more captures. But, before returning to his post, the tout would beckon to the advocate and they would go off together apparently to hold some secret conversation; of course, they were only going to settle accounts.

Afterwards, when all the bail matters had been disposed of and the judge had left, some touts would go for a drink at the nearest unauthorised bar. Even during court hours a couple of them appeared to be permanently drunk, and that too in the heat of a summer afternoon.

During one of these Sundays I struck up a friendship with Bihari. Mr Bihari was more than just an ordinary middleman.

Most of the soliciting he left to less able touts with whom he divided the fees. They came to him confident that he'd be able successfully to demand and charge five to six times the amount they would have been able to get on their own. Bihari also commissioned many lawyers who came to him requesting work.

You didn't often get to meet a conman like Bihari. He was in a class by himself. The way he was able to get clients to part with their money was remarkable. Confidence trickster par excellence is how I would describe him.

For some reason he took a liking to me, and we started working together. I began to understand many things about how our courts functioned. More important, I now had money to cover all my mother's medical expenses.

In his early forties, Bihari was white-haired with pasty white skin, owing to a disorder of some kind. Perfectly respectable-looking from the outside, he wore a spotless white safari suit each day of the week. The outfit had been chosen with care and for a reason that I did not comprehend immediately but came to understand over time. Apart from the fact that white is a symbol of purity and is a cool colour, his suit was designed to make the less-educated clients whom he accosted scratch their heads and wonder whether he was a lawyer or a judge.

India is such a hot country, but our stupid law-makers in their slavish imitation of the British have passed regulations requiring lawyers to wear the black coats and robes that are more appropriate to the English weather. In the Thirty Thousand Courts they often move around wearing just a white shirt over white, black or striped trousers, and they put on the coat and robes only when they enter a courtroom. As soon as they are out of the courtroom, they hand over their coat and robes to their *munshi*. So Bihari could pass for a lawyer in the eyes of some. But, by wearing a safari suit that was tailored differently, Bihari made sure that no one could point a finger at him and accuse him of attempting to impersonate a lawyer.

'Bihari, *bhai*,' I said to him one day. 'If you had an MBA you would have been Vice-President of Marketing for Coca-Cola or any of these big companies.'

'You know I don't like colas,' he smiled. 'Special tea with white cream floating on it is good enough for me.'

Money started to pour in as a result of my association with Bihari. I was able to clear huge loans incurred in paying for my father's treatment, and I could also now explore alternative therapies to save my mother's life.

* * *

Hope still survived. I took my mother to one of the big private hospitals, precursors of the five-star luxury hospitals that would soon emerge in new shining-bright India, catering to medical tourists unable to afford the high insurance premiums in the US. The experienced senior doctors there confirmed the earlier diagnosis. I then took her to an Ayurvedic Healing Centre in the Himalayas, and spent a lot of money on hakims and charlatans who promised a magic cure, but in the end all these efforts were to no avail.

My mother's cancer was at a final, advanced stage. The doctors advised chemotherapy, but explained that it wouldn't cure her – it would simply improve the quality of her life. By this, I guess they meant that she would suffer less pain. I was against chemotherapy, having seen the havoc it had wrought in my father's case, but my mother decided to opt for it. It's true that she didn't suffer much pain – at least Ruhno and I were never made aware of it, bless her soul – and then, just a week before the predicted six months, she too passed away.

I sometimes think that my mother developed her cancer as a kind of emotional reaction to my father's illness. Medically speaking this is pure nonsense, but the thought comes to my mind again and again.

After her death I stopped working with Bihari, taking on only regular cases. Sometimes, on an exceptional basis, we did some work together. And we continued to be friends.

13

As luck would have it, my friendship with Bihari was ultimately to resolve the problem of how to get Amit Patel removed from the White House.

After I'd tried to storm into his residence on the day I was arrested, having experienced an epiphany that he might have been an accomplice in Ruhno's rape, Amit seemed to realise that the *paan* leaf he had placed in his mouth was larger than he could chew. He beefed up security outside his residence. The White House became an impregnable fortress.

And security was similarly tightened at his office in Connaught Place, in the city centre. There were three or four bodyguards outside the building and a couple of them inside, posted at strategic points.

I've done some crazy things in my younger days, but I'm no James Bond and didn't even consider attempting to break through all that security to reach Amit. No, that would just have been too silly of me. And I may be stupid sometimes – I probably am – but I am certainly not that foolish.

The next few days passed in a blur. I went to the courts, argued my cases, returned to my apartment and did all the usual things. But I was preoccupied with my need for revenge. Justice is what I wanted, and despite being a lawyer – or perhaps because I was a lawyer – I had no faith in the ability of the courts to provide me with any kind of satisfaction. And yet by a supreme irony it was the men from the Thirty Thousand Courts, the place where I had spent the last twenty years of my life, who became my collaborators.

And the first of these was Bihari, confidence trickster par excellence. I had thought of going to him for advice but by a bizarre coincidence it was he who came to me.

* * *

In the middle of my musings about how to get hold of Amit Patel with all the security apparatus girdling him, Bihari turned up in my office one bright morning with a fat client.

'Please wait,' he instructed his client, entering my chambers and closing the door behind him. 'The poor man wants to evict his tenant.' He gave me a meaningful look.

'You know I don't do shady stuff any more.'

'An exclusive property in Golf Links,' he said, ignoring my comment. 'There are many lawyers but I need someone like you. Someone meticulous about details.'

I knew there was no shortage of other lawyers he could have hired. But I wasn't interested.

'There is a lot of money involved here.' He took a seat opposite me, withdrew a small steel container from his shirt pocket, and tapped some chewing tobacco into his mouth. 'Enough for us to buy the new Chevrolet on the market.'

Having regard for our long association, more out of politeness than anything else, I said: 'Whose property is this? Where in Golf Links?'

'A place called the White House,' he said, leaning across the table, a gleam in his eyes.

I stared at him in disbelief. 'Amit Patel?'

'That's the name.'

'I'll do it.' I trembled. An opportunity seemed to have come my way. By magic, almost.

'Some enmity?' He was alert to my changed expression.

I nodded.

'That's why I always say, "Never lose faith in God."'

A smile flitted across Bihari's face as he flung open the door and beckoned the owner of the property inside.

'*Namaskar, vakil sa'ab*. Greetings, Mr Lawyer.' The man entered with his hands folded in greeting.

I waved him to the chair next to Bihari's.

Kumar Jain was a tall, stooping man wearing a plain yellow bush shirt. His simple attire and drawn-out accent made me understand immediately that he belonged to the rich landed gentry from Old Delhi settled in the city for many years.

'Tea? Coffee?' I said. 'No cola for Mr Bihari, I know.'

I sent Hetram to fetch us some *mathis* and special teas – an extra dollop of cream thrown into Bihari's mug – from Saeed, my regular tea and biscuit supplier.

'It's simple enough.' Bihari paused to savour with evident relish the blob of cream that floated in his cup. 'Mr Kumar wants his property back. And his tenant, Mr Amit Patel' – he turned to his client – 'our lawyer knows him' – he shifted his gaze back to me – 'that *betichod* doesn't want to leave.'

'Mr Bihari has come highly recommended to us,' Kumar Jain said in a low voice. 'He helped my brother recover his property in Kashmiri Gate. Property that was stuck in litigation for . . . fifteen years.'

'Twenty,' threw in Bihari.

'And Bihari-ji tells me that you were the best person for this case – if you will only agree.'

'Might I ask why you want the property back?'

'Same old story. I've been asked to vacate the property where I myself am a tenant.'

'Why have you agreed? You know . . .' I dipped a *mathi* in the tea.

All over Delhi there were houses occupied by tenants who weren't leaving because the houses they themselves owned were in turn not being vacated by their tenants. This vicious circle afflicted thousands of properties. I expected Kumar Jain to know this.

'We are family,' Kumar Jain said.

'It's Jain *sa'ab*'s wife's brother who owns it,' Bihari elaborated. 'Can't refuse. He has agreed to vacate in six months. Three months left now. So Jain *sa'ab* wants his place back and has been pleading with Amit Patel. Amit told him to talk to his fancy lawyers at the Connaught Place office.'

'My dealings were with the late Sunil Gupta,' Kumar Jain said. 'There was a clear understanding that I would get the premises back in a year. It is stated in the agreement.'

'What you write in the agreement doesn't matter,' Bihari said.

Kumar Jain looked at me.

'Bihari is right,' I said. 'You can write whatever you want. The tenancy laws will override your agreement.'

Kumar Jain said, 'When the time came, I contacted Sunil, who asked me to speak to Amit.'

'And?'

'And Sunil quite coolly said that they weren't going to vacate. Go talk to Singhania and Kapoor, our company lawyers, he said.'

A few moments of silence.

'*Arre, ek* drink *marte hain*,' Bihari said. 'Let's go and grab a drink.'

We stepped out of my office and strolled past tables occupied by stamp vendors and notaries public, crossing over the street to enter one of the unlicensed bars on the other side of the gargantuan court building. Inside we took a private room. Bihari ordered whiskies and kebabs.

It's been done before, we told Kumar Jain, and it's been known to work.

'We will hand you the keys to your house,' Bihari said after the third drink. 'My personal guarantee. We'll take full payment only afterwards.'

* * *

In the Thirty Thousand Courts there are generally to be found a few reasonably well-to-do operators who specialise in obtaining *ex parte* eviction orders against recalcitrant tenants. These agents charge huge fees for their services – and my friend Bihari is one of the best in the business. Landlords are willing to dole out exorbitant sums because the stakes are high. In the millions. Property prices in New Delhi compare favourably with those in London and New York.

Amit Patel had been in India long enough to understand how difficult the tenancy laws were. You don't invest millions in real estate business without knowing this simple fact.

He was, however, relatively new to the system and might not have been aware of the extent to which apparently respectable property owners are willing to conspire with disreputable elements to get their own way. A landlord in Delhi even went to the length of having a Supreme Court eviction order forged. In some cases frustrated landlords have assaulted, and even attempted to murder, uncooperative tenants!

Bihari wasn't your run-of-the-mill confidence trickster who would take a landlord's money and disappear around the corner. Someone observing him in the bar with us might have thought he was a bit crazy, for once he starts drinking he speaks loudly with colourful abuse falling from his mouth like coins jumping out of a slot machine. But there's no madness in his methods. Over the years he has refined and perfected his *modus operandi*.

'I'll be getting on then,' said Bihari, as he swallowed the last of his drink. '*Vakil sa'ab* will explain everything to you, Mr Jain.'

* * *

'Come over to my chambers in the morning a little before ten, Mr Jain,' I said, once I had noted down details of the property. 'We'll file your case first thing as soon as the courts open.'

'What case?'

'An eviction petition.'

'On what grounds?'

'Oh, we'll throw in a few.'

'Such as?' Kumar Jain sounded deferential, not wanting to question my authority but unable to keep his curiosity at bay.

'Bona fide personal necessity, for one. This means that you want your property back for your own needs, not just to let it out again to someone else at a higher rent.'

'This is true.'

'So we will state the truth,' I said, 'but we'll also throw in "misuse of premises" for good measure.'

'Misuse?'

'Yes, he holds official meetings there sometimes, doesn't he?'

'Is that illegal?'

'You've let out the place to him for residential use. He can't be running his businesses from there, you see.'

'True.'

'So we'll give that as our second ground for eviction. And we'll also allege "unlawful subletting". We'll say he lets out rooms for visitors to stay in. Business associates, not family. Even if it's for a few days, that's not permitted under your agreement. We don't know if he's charging these people. That's illegal too.'

'Thank you, thank you.' Kumar Jain was suddenly all smiles. I understood that he had reached the moment when he was able to place full confidence in me. 'You need some . . .'

'Later.'

* * *

We filed the petition the following morning.

It came up in the afternoon before an Additional Rent Controller's court. Without glancing at me, almost routinely, the tired-looking judge issued notice to the tenant. Summonses, along with a copy of the petition, were to be dispatched by registered 'acknowledgement due' mail and also served personally by a court emissary.

'Something important for you to do, Hetram,' I said, once I was back in the chamber.

'*Sa'ab*?'

'Go over to the Process Serving Agency tomorrow morning. And find out who will be serving the summons in the White House eviction case.'

'*Sa'ab*.'

'And fix it that we have a report the next hearing that summons was refused.' I handed him 2000 rupees.

'You mean....' Hetram paused.

'I mean that he shouldn't bother with going there, but simply prepare a report saying that he went and they refused to accept the summons...'

Hetram smiled.

'Consider it done, *sa'ab*. But I'll confirm to you once the report is in.'

'Okay. Good. There is a second task. I want you to go across to the Lodi Road post office. In a day or so, they should be getting the registered envelope for delivery of summons to Amit.' I poured some water into a glass and sipped it. 'And fix the postman who goes there too.' I peeled out five 500-rupee notes and gave these to him.

'I'll let you know how it works out, sir – and bring back the change,' he said.

An honest *munshi*. Whoever heard of such a thing? But Hetram is honest, amazingly enough. Despite years traversing the corrupt corridors of these courts.

'Okay. Now bugger off somewhere and don't come back till tomorrow morning.'

Hetram smiled. He was happy to be given so much time off.

We suited each other.

* * *

'You have the report from the post office as well?' said the harried Rent Controller when the matter came up for hearing. He didn't bother to look up and continued to study the report given by the court emissary.

'Yes, Your Honour.' I pushed forward the envelope with the postman's scrawl that there was a refusal to accept delivery.

'Okay,' he said. 'Madam Steno, please type out . . .' And the court recorded its satisfaction that the tenant Amit Patel was deliberately and wilfully avoiding service, and passed an order directing that he be proceeded *ex parte*.

'Is the party here?' The judge looked up, realising that he could increase his score for decisions rendered that month.

'Waiting outside.'

'Record his statement, then. I'll pass orders before closing court.'

Kumar Jain came in and basically repeated everything that had already been averred in the petition. The steno punched away at the keyboard, sometimes listening, sometimes copying from the petition itself whenever she was unsure of an English word or legal expression, and it was done in half an hour, signatures and all.

By four o'clock we had the stamped copy of the eviction order.

Now to get the motherfucker evicted.

* * *

It was crucial to the scheme mapped out by us that Amit should remain unaware of the existence of the eviction order passed against him until the day he was actually dispossessed. Otherwise, even after the court had passed an *ex parte* order of eviction, Amit could rush to the court, move an urgent application alleging collusion with the serving agency on the part of Mr Kumar Jain, and secure a stay of operation of the eviction order.

I didn't want Amit to even be in the house the day we had him thrown out. I knew that his lawyers commanded considerable clout and we could be stopped even while executing court orders. Perhaps a partner in the law firm was a family friend of a Supreme Court justice. Having reached this far, I didn't want to be taking any more chances.

So I needed to know when Amit was out of town.

I knew he visited Bombay frequently.

I called his secretary. All the office numbers were stored in Ruhno's address book.

'Can I speak to Mr Amit Patel?' I said.

'Who is this?'

'I'm the Dean from the Bombay Institute of Management,' I said. 'I'm in Delhi for the day. I was hoping to be able to see Mr Patel tomorrow morning some time.'

I heard the woman consult someone.

'That won't be possible, I'm afraid. Mr Amit Patel's engagements over the next two days are full up.'

'That's fine,' I said. It was more or less what I had anticipated. 'But we – that's me and some of our Faculty – were hoping to meet Lord Patel during one of his visits to Bombay.'

'What is this about?'

'Oh, for him to come to our institute and lecture our students, just a couple of hours, nothing more.'

'You'll have to arrange that with the Bombay office, I'm afraid, sir.'

'Okay, so can you tell me when he'll be in Bombay next?'

'Where's Amit's appointments book?' I heard her ask someone. 'Oh, it's just here.' I heard the noise of the diary's pages being turned.

'He's there next week, sir.' She came back on the line 'The whole of next week in fact, sir. So I'm sure you can ask if he can spare you some time. But I suggest you call the Bombay office at once.'

So we had an entire week to get him out. Three days would have been enough.

* * *

Lest the proverbial cat be let out of the bag, the bailiff was slipped a fat bribe by Bihari on Kumar Jain's behalf for him to furnish a false report in court to the effect that, in pursuance of the court order, he had visited the premises but encountered resistance from Amit Patel. In reality he had not visited the premises, let alone met Amit – we had merely driven past in Kumar Jain's Mercedes so he could get an idea of the place.

We all sat not far from my chambers at the Thirty Thousand Courts in one of the better illegal pubs, drinking fine Scotch whisky – I am more flexible, and am open to a good Indian rum once in a while, but my friend Bihari doesn't like anything else – and, in between bites from the piping-hot kebabs that accompanied our drinks, Bihari and I cast a glance at the bailiff's draft report which was to the effect that Amit Patel had resisted eviction. While the bailiff savoured his samosas with green chutney, Bihari and I tweaked and fine-tuned his report to make it appear totally authentic.

On the basis of the bailiff's report filed the next day, on an application moved by me on behalf of the landlord, the court granted us police assistance after recording its satisfaction that, owing to resistance offered by Amit Patel, it was not possible to hand over the physical possession of the premises to the landlord in the absence of such aid.

* * *

'We need to have a brief chat with the Police SHO,' I said. 'Mr Jain, you need to come with me. Bring about, say, fifty thousand rupees.'

'All right, sir.'

The day before the planned eviction, Kumar Jain and I drove up to the Lodi Road police station under whose jurisdiction the White House property fell.

There were about a dozen people outside his office waiting to see him, but I knew my lawyer's robes would fast-track my entry. So we breezed past them.

'Jetley. Ajay Jetley.' The Station House Officer stood up to shake hands with me. He was in his mid-thirties and athletic. His personality radiated aggression combined with a practical, world-weary awareness. 'What can I do for you, *vakil sa'ab*?'

I showed him the court order.

'Will be done, sir. Tomorrow?'

'In the morning, if possible.'

'*Jab kaho*. Always prompt to follow court directions.'

'Thank you.' I turned to Kumar Jain. 'This is Mr Jain, the property owner. He'd like to thank you.'

Kumar Jain looked a bit scared, not knowing what to do.

'*Arrey* Jain *sa'ab*,' Jetley said. 'Listen to what your lawyer says.' He turned to an assistant who sat at a table in the corner typing something. '*Oye*, Shetty.'

'Yes, sir.' The man stopped his work.

'Could you just leave us for five minutes?'

The man stood up without a word and prepared to exit.

'And shut the door behind you. And don't let anyone else enter. We have something confidential to discuss.'

Kumar Jain now took out a bulky envelope and gingerly proffered it to the policeman.

He took it, opened it and did a quick count.

'Estimate a bit on the lower side, *vakil sa'ab*.'

'Just an advance,' I said.

He laughed at that. 'Okay, I'm not a greedy person,' he said. 'Just give me the same amount once again and we'll consider it a deal.'

I turned to Kumar.

'Haven't brought any more,' he mumbled.

'Doesn't matter,' said the policeman. 'We have *vakil sa'ab*'s guarantee. That's good enough for me. Coffee? Coke? *Kya chalega*?'

A little later when he walked us to the door of his cavernous office, before opening it he turned to me and said, 'The thing is, *vakil sa'ab*, as you very well know, everyone is on the take. The difference is what you take the take for. For me, I only believe in doing good things.'

We thanked him and left.

* * *

So it happened that on the fateful day Kumar Jain, the landlord, and Bihari arrived at Amit Patel's Golf Links residence complete with bailiff, police party, some casual labour and, I believe, even a truck or two in tow.

What next? Under the watchful eyes of a curious neighbourhood, Amit Patel's eviction from the White House was rapidly and mercilessly effected. The furniture and household goods that belonged to him were placed on the roadside pavement. Everybody turned a deaf ear to the pleas and entreaties of the bewildered servants and security guards that they might be given some time to contact their employer and at least remove his effects to a proper place. Meanwhile, their master Amit was out of town, possibly discussing the acquisition of prime real estate in New Bombay.

I would have given a lot to have seen Amit Patel's expression when he returned to Delhi and found all his fancy furniture in a warehouse somewhere in Old Delhi.

The noose was tightening.

14

Once I had dealt with Amit Patel, I became more aware of Ruhno's absence and my solitary existence.

Life without Ruhno would never be the same. I hated coming back home to my apartment at night, but there was no choice. And so I didn't spend much time there after I finished work at the Thirty Thousand Courts. Rather, once court hours were over I chose to escape to the Delhi Sports Club in South Delhi, where I played a few hands of bridge or rummy, and then made my way to Sixers or Madhushala, two excellent bars within the premises. I would sit with some club cronies, have a few whiskies, some small snacks that also served as my evening meal, and then I would drive back to my apartment in Mukherjee Nagar around eleven.

I found it difficult to relax at home, since my next-door neighbour, Mrs Ahuja, liked to watch television serials in the evenings with the volume turned up because she and her husband had grown a little deaf with age. The apartment walls were so thin that someone coughing could easily be heard in an adjacent apartment.

That's why I went off to play bridge and drink whisky at the Delhi Sports Club on a regular basis. When the club was closed, I sometimes took a walk in a nearby park, to get some exercise and find some peace.

* * *

With Ruhno's death, the meaning had gone out of my life. As I walked round the park, I reminisced about the past. About Ruhno and her growing-up years.

Every now and then we would have a long weekend on account of a festival or lawyers' strike – lawyers' strikes in the Thirty Thousand Courts in the eighties and nineties were almost as frequent as festivals. I would take the *Himalayan Queen* early on a Friday morning, treating it as a holiday, reach Shimla by late evening, spend Saturday and Sunday with Ruhno, and be back in Delhi in time for the court cases scheduled for Monday morning.

Aside from my sister and my mother before her, there was no other woman in my life that I had ever really cared for. One evening as I sat on a park bench my eyes filled with tears when I thought once again of the terrible way that my sister had died, even as I reflected that it wasn't strictly true that there had been no other woman.

There had been Uma, a colleague at the Faculty of Law, at Delhi University. After we graduated, Uma worked as a junior lawyer for a large law firm in the Supreme Court. They did not pay her well, but in a few years she would make contacts and start doing much better. And slowly, slowly, things would improve and get better still. That was the way it worked, we all realised. Time and again Uma had tried to persuade me too to start a practice in that court.

'Don't practise law in the Thirty Thousand Courts,' she'd begged me. 'Please. For our sake.' And then she had voiced her real concern. 'If you continue there for much longer you'll become just a commoner.'

The words 'just a commoner' – one of hundreds of faceless lawyers with little income or reputation – rang in my ears for several days, but at the time I needed to start contributing financially to my family's household as soon as possible, so as I saw it I simply had no choice in the matter. But Uma either didn't appreciate my situation or didn't want to understand it, although I'd tried to explain it to her on a couple of occasions.

When I ruminate on my relationship with Uma, as I sometimes do in my quieter, lonelier moments, away from the hustle and bustle of the courtrooms, I tend to believe that she was attracted to me while we were both at the Faculty of Law only because I was one of the brightest students in class, and could on that basis be presumed to have a bright future. Perhaps I'm being bitter. I'm sure it wasn't as cut and dried as I'm making it out to be, and she probably did like me a lot, but I believe she couldn't bear the thought of being intimately associated with someone based in the Thirty Thousand Courts.

In the end, we quarrelled. Her parting words were spoken in a low, angry tone.

'So you will not understand. Well, then, I'd better be going. And I don't think I'll be coming back to see you.' She stood up haughtily.

As she walked out of the door, she turned to face me one last time, somehow summoned up a too-stretched smile, its fakery and purpose apparent, designed to hurt me as hard as possible, and uttered the following words, which echoed in my brain weeks after the event:

'You'll always remain what you are at present. A lowly Thirty Thousand Courts lawyer.'

But I didn't let her have the parting shot. I felt insulted and humiliated, but even then had the presence of mind to respond.

'Well, Uma,' I said. 'I'm sorry to learn that this is how you feel. But do you know something? Nobody in the larger world' – by this I meant outside India – 'has ever heard of the Thirty Thousand Courts. But one day these courts will be famous around the world. And do you know why? Because' – and I paused for dramatic effect – 'because they will say . . . that I practised here.'

She was momentarily speechless, surprised at the quickness and, dare I say it, the cleverness of my response. Recovering her composure, she then stood still, with the smile on her lips fading and the expression hardening, snorted contemptuously and walked away.

I don't know where those words came from. I am not psychic, although I have in my younger days, as we all have, pretended to read the hands of girls and women, as an excuse to be able to hold them. But I do believe today that those words I uttered were prophetic, and that in some way, because of me and what will soon happen, the Thirty Thousand Courts will become famous all around the world.

Ultimately, though, Uma married Kishore, a lawyer practising in the High Court. Kishore had studied with us in college but was more or less a second-rater with consistently poor grades. Uma had not so much as cast an eye on him during that period, but later on things changed. Kishore's father, who was still in government service as an income tax commissioner, had amassed wealth by taking huge bribes during an illustrious career in the civil service. So he managed to set up his son with his own private office in the Bengali Market area – which happens to be one of the truly posh areas in town, being close to Connaught Place as well as just a few minutes' drive from the Supreme Court and the High Court. It is the most favoured place for lawyers to have an office, but, whereas most lawyers manage to get an office there towards the middle of their careers, Kishore had three large rooms to set himself up in right at the beginning.

Uma and Kishore's marriage was troubled right from the start. They fought often, so I heard through my sources, and, despite producing two children, Uma was never really happy with the decision she had made. Not because Kishore wasn't a loving husband, not because he was not willing to indulge her, but because Uma actually needed a husband who would lead her, and that was something that Kishore was incapable of. Even physically he couldn't lead her, for she was taller than him by a couple of inches and a fast walker. I did encounter them occasionally in the High Court or the Supreme Court, which I visited off and on, and a couple of times I saw her with Kishore walking very rapidly to attend a court hearing, but he was clearly making an effort to keep pace with her. She walked with long strides, and I recalled that when we had been in college as an 'almost couple' I had refused to increase my pace to match hers; instead, she had slowed down to adjust to mine. This notion of the 'almost couple', which exists perhaps only in India, entailed in those days the suppression of all public displays of feeling and the containment of any private exhibition of lust beyond, say, the occasional stolen kiss, hug and grope until family approvals were firmly in place, a concession to the institution of the arranged marriage.

In the course of one of my drinking sessions with my friend Prem Sharma, he gave me a succinct analysis of what had happened, as he saw it. 'The thing is', he said, as he sipped the contents of what must have been the fifth or sixth glass of Johnny Walker Red Label (Prem can drink like a fish), 'you loved Uma, Kishore loved Uma too, Uma loved you but' – and here he had paused, giving me a serious and meaningful look – 'but Uma' – draining the contents of the glass of whisky in a dramatic gesture – 'but Uma married Kishore instead!' He had laughed, and I'd joined in, because many years had now passed, and by then I was beyond any bitterness. I have to say that's probably how it did happen. Uma doubtless loved me in her own way – but then again she loved the promise of the good life, as well as the good life itself, more than she ever loved me, or perhaps more than she was capable of loving any person apart from herself.

* * *

In the time that Ruhno had been away, as can be expected, I had had a couple of liaisons with women. It may surprise someone who hasn't visited India for a while that this is possible with respectable educated ladies. Well, India is changing. My first relationship was with a beautiful Bengali girl married to a communist revolutionary who spent most of his time travelling through the country 'networking', as he called it, with like-minded people, trying to bring about a red revolution in the country. Her name was Parvati and the man's name was Jyoti.

I first met Jyoti in the Thirty Thousand Courts, through Bihari, who accosted him while he was being taken to court by the police for an extension of his remand. Jyoti, poor fellow, had been arrested while putting up revolutionary posters in the dead of night, and had been charged under sections 91 and 92 of the Delhi Police Act with vagrancy and defacing public property. He was rather pleased to have been arrested. It confirmed several of his views about the nature of the Indian state, which he later told me about at length, after I had managed to get him released completely free of charge. Yes, I filed his papers, appeared on his behalf and secured his release – all this without any payment whatsoever. It was Bihari's assessment that the boy was from a 'good family', and that he would ultimately repay us for the effort. And so he did. We were hailed as revolutionary comrades, introduced to his colleagues, to his ailing mother with whom he lived in a first-floor apartment above Gol Market, or the Round Market, not five minutes away from Connaught Place. And I was introduced to Parvati, with the shining kohl-ringed eyes, and we knew from a first glance at each other that we clicked. So, during Jyoti's travels through the north, south, east and west of India, Parvati and I met frequently – first at her place, where I pretended I had come mainly to see her mother, and then at my place, when she would make an excuse that she was going to see some revolutionary friends.

We had a good few years, until one fine day Jyoti came to the realisation that all his travels across the country and his networking weren't helping the revolution much, and he decided to return to Delhi to try to make a revolution from the capital of the country. Parvati and I discussed our relationship and his return, and we agreed voluntarily to part ways. It wasn't easy, but it was best.

* * *

My second liaison was a relationship with Ujala, a professor of philosophy, no less, from a prestigious girls' college at Delhi University.

I had represented her in divorce proceedings against her husband. A rich businessman, Sandeep had turned violent a year after their marriage. The doctors diagnosed him as a paranoid schizophrenic. He was generally aggressive towards all and sundry, more especially towards the staff who worked for him. But towards Ujala he had been unquestionably tender for the first nine months of their marriage. The paranoid side to his personality had then asserted itself, and he began to imagine that his wife was having affairs with her colleagues at the university and with her boss the Dean, who had granted her what he suspected was an out-of-turn promotion. Sandeep even imagined her – and accused her of – having sex with his brother and father. Her protests served only to convince him further that he was right. He hammered her with his fists, abusing her loudly all the while, his tirades – which even the neighbours, could hear – drowning her screams. The family intervened, and he had to be forcibly controlled and temporarily institutionalised. Divorce in India is often a painful, prolonged affair, but the medical certificates provided by doctors were a great help, and I did manage to get her a divorce in record time – three and a half years.

During those three and a half years while the case dragged on, Ujala came to see me at least fifteen or twenty times, so we got to know each other pretty well. The day she was granted a divorce, she invited me home for a meal. And after the meal we got pretty close. Physically, I mean. And then we were together, more or less, for the next four years. Her house was not far from the courts, so after court hours I would turn up at her house. She had a small son, who would be sent out to play when I arrived. I never stayed overnight, for the neighbours would have talked. Our pretext was that we were writing a book on legal philosophy together. I'm sure that not all the neighbours accepted this excuse, but in India it is often sufficient that you present a reason, and, to be fair, it was not a bizarre idea. It was in fact credible, since Ujala had published quite a few articles in scholarly journals such as the *Indian Journal of Philosophy* and had even edited a couple of books on Indian philosophy.

After the divorce, her husband's mental health began to improve rapidly. I wonder sometimes whether it is the institution of marriage that provokes insecurity and suspicion. The same people, if they were living together in a relationship outside marriage, might not be so mistrustful or jealous. My theory may not have general applicability, but it certainly seemed to work as far as Ujala's husband was concerned, for six months after the divorce Sandeep began to make reconciliatory gestures.

I had met him in court on a few occasions, and despite his violent history with his wife he had always been well behaved there. My impression of him was of a highly intelligent man with a mental illness. He successfully ran a motor parts business, he made a lot of money, and he paid Ujala alimony throughout the proceedings; then later, when they were divorced, he voluntarily increased the amount.

At the weekends Sandeep came to the house to see his son. Ujala didn't invite him in. He arrived at a pre-set time, and when she heard the sound of his car horn, and saw from the window of her first-floor apartment that his car had arrived, she sent her son Bunty outside. I got along well with Bunty; he liked me and I liked him, but certainly his father loved him more, as he in turn loved his father.

There was a great irony in the situation. During the whole time they were married he suspected Ujala of having multiple affairs behind his back while he was working hard at his business, and all the while the poor woman was innocent of any wrongdoing, so I believe. And then when they did get divorced and we started to have a physical relationship – I'm sure there was little doubt in his mind that we were not writing a book together – he began to accept our affair. He realised he had wrongly suspected her of infidelity in the past and hoped for forgiveness. He wanted her back and promised that he would now behave and never again be violent.

On my part, in my relationship with Parvati I was strongly involved emotionally, whereas my affair with Ujala was mostly about sex.

Ujala did have a voracious sexual appetite, and on the few occasions when we managed to go to Haridwar or Rishikesh for a secret weekend, as soon as she was done with the visits to the bathing *ghats* and the temples, and we were back in the hotel, she would turn on me like a famished tigress. After the first such visit I made sure I took some aphrodisiacs, given to me by Hetram. They were very useful indeed, much better than all this Viagra stuff, about which there is so much hype. The thing is that Viagra gets you up and running, but it doesn't keep you running. A couple of laps and, like it or not, you're finished, but this stuff – it's like those steroids some of the athletes use.

Hetram, bless his soul, had really picked up a lot of useful information from the years he had spent with the Ayurvedic dispensary, and, had he but a fraction of the skills that Bihari possessed in selling himself, he would have been a rich man indeed. Instead he has chosen to work for me for a pittance that is a notch higher than the market rate for *munshis*!

Ujala didn't consider me seriously as a prospective husband, even though as a result of my efforts she was now free to marry, and the reason for this, plain and simple, was that I just didn't earn enough. She was a luxury-loving woman who liked the finer things of life, such as good cars, expensive perfumes and designer clothing.

Her ex-husband had enough money, on the other hand, and he wooed her consistently.

By some strange timing, barely weeks before Ruhno was due to return to live with me in Delhi on a permanent basis, Ujala called me one day to tell me that she had decided to go back to Sandeep. She hoped I would accept her decision, which she was taking for Bunty's benefit. I knew that for her there was the avoidance of the stigma that a divorced woman in

India still carries as well as the added attraction of luxurious living that she missed. I was angry and disappointed that she hadn't thought of consulting me before deciding, but Ruhno's anticipated return softened the blow in some inexplicable fashion, and on the whole I think I took it pretty well.

* * *

The past was replaying in my mind as I strolled out of the park.

I don't believe I would have conceded even to myself my need for a companion – I am too proud – if Ruhno hadn't died. I needed someone, but I knew that now no one could ever fill the void. With Ruhno's death, I found myself floating in a sea of desolation, with anguish bubbling up again and again. To get away from that sometimes unbearable pain, I needed to hit out. And I decided I would hit out, no matter what the cost.

Part Seven
Lunch

15

Oh, do have some more of this spicy chicken curry, Lord Patel. I can see you are quite startled by the exciting flavours. Perhaps you are wondering if this is another area your giant conglomerate can move into. A chain of Indian restaurants serving curries like this one, served with giant crispy *naans*? No?

I'm so glad you agreed to join me here at Nathu's. I come to eat here quite often. It's one of the *dhabas*, the low-priced eateries, that you find all over the country. When we entered, Lord Patel, I noticed you surveying the shabby interior as though you were planning a refurbishment. I saw you looking at the rough-hewn wooden chairs, the tables made of planks, the lack of tablecloths. White plates as thick as your finger and aluminium tumblers were slammed in front of us by one of the harried waiters rushing about, responding to shouts from customers for more *roti* or *dhal*. Nathu's caters mostly for lorry and taxi drivers but the food is fit for kings.

Yes, you're impatient to learn anything I know about your son, but be reassured, Lord Patel – I will tell you everything I know about your son, even his whereabouts. All in good time, my dear sir. After lunch.

What say we have a plate of *rasmalai* each? You hesitate. Perhaps you wonder if a place such as this would be able to prepare delicious desserts, even if it can rustle up a fantastic chicken curry? Fear not. The *rasmalai* is not made here, but across the street.

Yes, Lord Patel, that shop across the street, the sweet house, and you will note that it has the same name: Nathu's. That's where the *mathis* came from this morning. The shop was set up by this restaurant owner for his son. Just as you wanted your son to have his own fiefdom within the corporate empire that you created in less than two decades, so too Nathu, the owner of this *dhaba*, wanted his son to have a business of his own. Isn't the world so similar all over, Lord Patel? I have to say the son's shop is doing very well, and I'm sure his father's guidance has proved invaluable.

Ah, the *rasmalai* has come! Take a bite and tell me what you think. You like it! What did I tell you?

You know, the reason why traditional Indian women like my sister Ruhno can get trapped in a relationship with someone unsuitable – I can see you are getting worked up, my dear sir, but wait for me to finish and I think you'll agree with my assessment eventually – is because they are innocent and easy to seduce. How could I blame my sister for falling in love with your son? How could I blame her for her lack of discernment? Haven't we all had stupid crushes on people who don't deserve our attention?

I saw the signs before I broached the subject one dinnertime. There was something different about her during the meal. This *rasmalai*, which my sister knew was my favourite dessert, reminds me of the flush in her cheeks, the lilt in her voice, the exaggerated care with which she fed me the sweet dish. *Oh, my God*, I remember thinking, *my beloved Ruhno is in love!*

Shall we order another plate? No, you are full! You say that it compares most favourably with the excellent *rasmalai* that you've tasted at Brilliant's in Southall, London. Well, thank you!

You have eaten so well, perhaps, because I've told you that you'll learn your son's whereabouts before the day ends. Your patience or perhaps paternal love has won out.

After Ruhno dismissed my concerns about Amit, she no longer told me everything the way she used to, because she was in love with a man I didn't like. She had stopped listening to me. And so, my dear sir, not knowing what to do, a year ago I decided to meet you.

The Indian newspapers had all announced beforehand that you were coming to India, you would meet with the Indian Prime Minister, the Finance Minister and captains of Indian industry, who were worried about your takeovers. I knew you'd stay with your son.

India is changing, but much of India remains the same, and some of it is good. Do you remember, Lord Patel, that these were your words when I went to meet you just one year ago? I had come to talk about the relationship developing between your son and my sister. To request you to ask your son to be careful with her.

You greeted me warmly, almost as though you'd been expecting me, and you didn't bat an eyelid when I introduced myself as the brother of Ruhno, your son's friend. You seemed a bit uneasy, but remained impeccably courteous when I explained how I was concerned for my sister's situation in the relationship that was developing between her and your son.

You heard me out and then you pronounced your judgement.

You said you had met my sister, and knew that she was Amit's friend and also did some work for his company. They were both adults and we shouldn't really interfere in their affairs.

There was little I could reply to that. You were right.

But you see, Lord Patel, you didn't say anything that was very different from what I expected. There was a faint irrational hope in my mind that you would take the matter seriously enough to try to persuade your son to have an engagement with Ruhno if he was at all honourable, but before coming to your house that day I had estimated that it was far more likely that you would say, in the modern Indian way, that they were getting to know each other, and surely we should allow them to decide what was best for them. I even thought you might say – which you did actually say – that if I was that worried I would do better to speak to my sister than ask you to speak to your son.

I believed it would be worthwhile to meet you and speak with you, even if you reacted as I suspected you would, because I judged that you would at least tell your son about my visit and my concerns, and that that in itself would put up a kind of barrier to any dishonourable intentions that your son might have had towards Ruhno. I thought it might act as a kind of curb on his actions, you see.

I was so impressed by your personality and the way you spoke that I nearly changed my mind about your son. I thought that a man like yourself must surely have a worthy son. And then I reminded myself that quite often worthy men have worthless sons.

And therefore when I went home I did try hard once again to convince Ruhno, but I knew she wasn't really listening. She was flying high, my little darling. And nothing I could say, no eloquence on my part, no dramatic monologues, could have convinced her, at that point in time, of the truth of what I was saying. I knew she wasn't listening to me, but I hoped that she would not resume seeing Amit, at least at a personal, intimate level. But that's what she did!

If you will excuse me for a moment, I'll go around the corner to ease myself. Nature's calls can be delayed but not avoided, and I'll leave you alone, for a few minutes – for you to stew in your own juice.

* * *

Some coffee, Lord Patel? Yes? I have just ordered two espresso coffees from the waiter, Harish. I think he will bring them from the sweet shop across the street, so it may take a while. The waiter is a friend of mine. I sometimes pass some business his way. What business? Oh well, court business, if you must know. I'll tell you about that a bit later.

Here we are, Lord Patel – Indian-style espresso, with chocolate powder spattered over the foam. As you know, I'm a tea drinker mainly, but I too, just like you it appears, enjoy coffee after a meal.

Nine months ago, when Amit didn't turn up at the office one day, your people were not too surprised. Why do you think that was the case? Because he was a bit of a philanderer? Perhaps he's caught up with some woman, they might have thought.

My guess is that, when he didn't show up the next day as well, senior management in the company got worried. For Amit did think of himself as a playboy of sorts, but also as a serious professional businessman, and it was uncharacteristic of him to suddenly disappear. Phone calls would have been made to everyone who knew him, both in India and overseas. The last time he'd been seen was in the lobby of the Hyatt Regency, talking to the man at the reception desk.

On the third day of his disappearance, your company's people decided to tell you. And then the press also got hold of the story. No one knew what had happened.

You left everything, didn't you? All your business meetings, engagements with high-powered people that often include prime minister and presidents, and flew across to New Delhi to try to get to the bottom of the matter.

And like any good investigator you called all the staff at the office and personally interviewed each person. And you did the same also with the staff at home: the housekeeper, the cook, the cleaners, and the security staff at the entrance to the house.

And my guess is that it was not until then that Balram, that sloppily dressed paunchy security guard, told you about my visit and the threat I'd directed to your son, Amit, to drag him out of his hiding place and kill him. I'd even indicated that this would happen before the festival of Holi.

You had a very poor witness, Lord Patel, and I think I managed to discredit him completely. In Indian courts it is common for counsel to make suggestions to a witness. If the witness has been properly briefed, he understands that it is routine for counsel to suggest that he is telling lies, and he has to be relaxed and reply politely and even matter-of-factly that no, he is not telling lies. Your witness started to shout.

The guard had not been briefed even on this elementary aspect by the lawyers from Singhania and Kapoor.

And then I produced my own witnesses. I produced our waiter, Harish. See how he is enjoying a break, smoking a *bidi* at the edge of the restaurant to keep the smoke out while he himself remains protected from the sunlight. You obviously don't have such a good memory for faces as you have for figures.

Allow me let to you in on one of the small secrets of the legal profession in India, Lord Patel. We can hire witnesses who are trained to tell lies. And they are better than any of our Bollywood – or shall I say even Hollywood – actors.

Oh, Lord Patel, will you have some of these sweetened fennel seeds? Or some *mishri*, these sugar crystals that sparkle like diamonds?

The week before the trial, Bihari had dropped by my chambers in connection with several civil cases that Kumar Jain, a satisfied client, had wanted me to file, and I had asked him for help in obtaining two witnesses for my case. He had promised to get hold of Sikander, the gardener – who did actually know something about plants, and had worked as a gardener before, though not with Delhi University – and he suggested I contact Harish directly, as I did.

I see you're finding all this difficult to digest. Have you ever read the crime fiction author Agatha Christie, Lord Patel? Yes? You'll remember how, in Agatha Christie's novels, Hercule Poirot has this knack of turning up at places where murders occur soon after his arrival. On the last day, Poirot delivers a lengthy exposition of how the crimes have been committed, leading to the final revelation. Up to that moment, his audience must listen and be patient.

In criminal trials, our court witnesses are sometimes numerically far ahead – they are witnesses to hundreds of thefts, accidents, robberies and killings.

So many things you don't know, Lord Patel. But really, you shouldn't be upset that you lost the case. The only difference it would have made is that, had the court asked the police to prosecute me, I might have been arrested by them and kept in their lock-up for a few days before being sent to prison. During the period I was in their custody the police would have tortured me. The way your son tried to have me tortured. Don't you know about that?

I see from your expression that you know about the episode.

And didn't you yourself want the police to arrest me on kidnapping charges – and torture me?

Come now, Lord Patel, we are all grown-ups here. Why would you waste time and money filing a complaint if you could get the police to act right away?

You saw how lawyers in Pakistan brought down the government, didn't you?

It's the same here. We lower-court lawyers are a powerful lot. The Commissioner wouldn't have dared. But the police would have tortured me if the judge had authorised prosecution.

But I don't know how much this would have helped you because I'd have been out on bail soon enough. In a few days. Bail, not jail, that's the clear Supreme Court ruling. And after that . . .

Your case would have dragged on for another six years. Maybe eight years. And then there would have been the possibility of an appeal, a second appeal.

Lord Patel, the delays in your complaint were nothing. You had entered a justice system where cases are filed by one generation and verdicts received by the next. There was nothing for me to worry about, even had you been successful. The day of our hearing – do you know how many cases were listed for hearing that afternoon? Thirty-five. All adjourned by three months. That's why lawyers refer to the courts as date-giving machines. .

Ah, Lord Patel, I think that we now need to change the venue of our discussion. We've enjoyed a hearty meal at Nathu's – something you didn't expect, I'm certain, given your first impression of the front of the restaurant and its interior decor. You wonder, Lord Patel, don't you, why the food here is so much more tasty than the five-star cuisine you've been sampling at the Taj Palace, the five-star hotel where you're staying. Well, that food can simply never match up to what is on offer at Nathu's. You ask why? Well, I'll let you in on a secret. It's all about the poor quality of stocks that the Taj Palace is dealing in. You smile. But, Lord Patel, it's not stocks and shares that I am talking about, though I'm not surprised that that was your first inference. I'm talking about the stock curry that's put in the food in the kitchen at a five-star hotel. They use the same for each of the fifty dishes they have on the menu, while here you have only three main dishes on offer and each of them stews in its own juices.

Where shall we go? Should we head back to my chambers? I think not. I have a better suggestion. Let's go to a bar.

You raise your eyebrows in surprise at my suggestion. Can a bar be found anywhere in this ramshackle marketplace? Yes, indeed, although it may not exactly match the description of the Board Room at Delhi Sports Club.

It's not far from here. Just a short ten-minute walk and we'll be there. Come, come, and as we walk I'll tell you about these illegal bars that lie hidden away in alleys forking off the main street that runs parallel to the Thirty Thousand Courts. The first time I visited one of these, many years ago, I was also surprised to learn of their existence.

Will we be breaking the law? Yes, I suppose we will. Is there any chance of being arrested? None at all. These were the very questions I asked myself, when I first entered the precincts of one of these places. As soon as I entered I saw the reassuring presence of two policemen tossing back glasses of *santara*, the locally brewed stuff that was so popular in those days.

You will not drink, you say, but will accompany me. Have no worries, Lord Patel. I don't propose that you drink *santara*, *mausami* or any of the local liquors that are manufactured illegally in the city and on its outskirts. There is a generic term that is applied to all such liquids: *tharra*. I suppose you could call *tharra* a kind of country liquor, but it is much harsher in its taste, and sometimes it can prove highly dangerous. Every year there are reports of a few hundred people having gone blind or even died after consuming bottles of this illegally manufactured liquor. Why do people drink it then? Oh well, it's a fraction of the price you would pay for a bottle of properly refined liquor. No taxes to the central or state government, you see. Only bribes paid to policemen and local authorities to make sure that these activities of preparing and distributing the *tharra* go on unhindered.

Anyhow, Lord Patel, have no fear. I wouldn't dream of consuming any of these suspicious, spurious liquids. We'll have a wide range of choices, and the three principal categories will be *tharra*, which I've already explained to you; *desi*, which is the legal, locally manufactured Indian brew; and *videshi*, which means of course imports that include your Johnny Walkers and other kinds of Scotch whisky. You look relieved. Oh, you won't be drinking yourself, but you're relieved for my sake. How kind of you, sir. You may look Indian, but truly you are a British gentleman. I can see there was good reason for the Queen to bestow a knighthood on you. You are a man of charm and distinction, a knight errant even, as in the

Middle Ages, for you have travelled widely and duelled with many an adversary. Although it's true of course that your adventures have taken place in the modern, corporate world.

Your son too believed in adventures, but of a different kind, and unlike you he made many mistakes. Including one . . . should I say . . . fatal error?

Part Eight
Cocktails

16

Ah, we are here already, sir. I didn't even notice the time it took us to walk to this place. You are amused at the signboard. Yes, it's called 'Johnny's'. Surprising name, is it? Tejinder Singh, the Sikh owner of this 'pub' – what is the difference between a bar and a pub, by the way? I've never been able to understand that distinction – is a great fan of a Bollywood star of yesteryear, someone called Dev Anand, , and Dev Anand once starred in a blockbuster movie called *Mera Naam Johnny*, or *My Name is Johnny*, in which he played the role of a westernised Indian detective. Anyway, Tejinder loved that movie so much that he saw it eleven times. And so, when he opened this bar he decided to name it 'Johnny's'. You don't watch Bollywood, you say. Only Hollywood. And that, too, very occasionally. Well, I'm sure in your youth you must have seen a John Wayne film. You have? Well then, it's easy to explain it to you. Dev Anand is, quite simply, the John Wayne of Bollywood.

You don't agree that this place, this illegal drinking place, qualifies as an Indian version of an English pub? On reflection, I probably agree with you. They are playing ghazals on the tape, a soft lyrical kind of music that goes well with drinking and speculation. You don't have, to my knowledge, an equivalent kind of music that accompanies a peaceful drink, which merges the very act of drinking with nostalgia, romance and even philosophical speculation. You see, in our culture there is a degree to which drinking is romanticised. This is so all over the eastern world, I guess, which is why the *Rubaiyat of Omar Khayyam* must have seemed so exotic and otherworldly when British poets first read it.

But, apart from the kind of music being played here, the other reason I agree with you is that in this place there are no women. It's very much an all-male affair. In the English pub, by contrast, many of the customers are women, often as part of a couple, or in groups, rarely on their own; some even come hoping to encounter a new boyfriend. You crinkle your nose in disapproval, disagreement and disgust. Have I assessed your expression correctly? Yes. Well, sir, this was certainly my experience the one time I visited your mother country. I do grant this is not the norm, and it's true that it was a long while ago, but at the time some of my friends and I had done what in colloquial English you refer to as a 'pub crawl'. And as we imbibed beer after beer and made our progress through certain select pubs scattered across the city – not the classy ones that someone like you would deign to visit, not even the respectable working- and middle-class pubs you wouldn't bother going to – we saw places that were a flesh market, a cattle market of sorts, where young and middle-aged British women (as well as ethnic Indian women in some places, mind you) were open, even eager, to being approached by men. You disagree with me. Well, let's not labour the point any further. We can simply agree to disagree. Isn't that a nice turn of phrase? Suffice it to say that this place here, this Indian illegal drinking place, call it what you will, doesn't cater for any women, either of the commercial or the non-commercial variety.

Not to say that you wouldn't find some women doing hanky-panky stuff a stone's throw away. You'd just need a good arm. You see, Lord Patel, when you came to my chambers in the morning you felt disgusted, didn't you, by the shabby surroundings, the sordid atmosphere. As compared with the Supreme Court lawyers' complex, or even the Delhi High Court lawyers' complex, the lawyers' chambers complex in the Thirty Thousand Courts, in terms of atmosphere, is as distant as the moon is from the earth, if not from the sun.

But there are different levels of shabbiness and sordidness. My office is located in what is commonly referred to as the 'civil side' of the court complex, which if not less shabby is certainly less sordid than what is referred to as the 'criminal side'. You found the civil side deserted today, didn't you? That would not have been the case with the chambers constructed on the criminal side. There would have been a fair buzz of activity there, even today, on a Sunday, when the courts are mostly shut down.

What kind of activity, you will no doubt ask. Well, there are some chambers where there will be an open bottle of whisky placed on the lawyer's desk, with four or five lawyers and sometimes a colleague imbibing their spirits together with some French fries, some crisps, possibly even some chicken tikkas purchased from Nathu's, where we have just had lunch. I don't favour drinking in the chambers, which is the reason, Lord Patel, that I have brought you here; otherwise drinking in my chambers was certainly a viable option.

Anyhow, to resume, in some of the chambers on the criminal side there will be drinking and drinking alone.

In some other chambers there will be a drinking and gambling group. So, drinks accompanied by the various savouries, and everybody playing cards in deadly earnest. The level of the game is quite high, I can assure you. We even have some professional gamblers who come over and beg to be allowed to play, 'to keep in training', as they call it.

There are the drinking and talking groups, and then there are the drinking and gambling (no talking please) groups, and then there are the three lawyers and a hooker groups as well. Yes, there is hanky-panky business with women going on, just as we speak, not far away from where we are sitting.

There is a major red light area, Delhi's biggest prostitution centre, known as the GB Road area, which falls within the jurisdiction of the Thirty Thousand Courts. The way the law works in India is that a 'lady of the night' (even though some of these places are much like your 24/7 call centres) cannot be arrested for prostitution, but she can be arrested for soliciting. A fine distinction, you could say, but, as you well know, the law is full of such niceties. Loopholes in the law, you might call them. Anyhow, in practice the establishments that provide sex workers – yes, that's a better term than prostitutes, isn't it? – continue to run their businesses just so long as the monthly pay-offs reach the police stations, the gangs and the politicians, but even then now and again a few women are rounded up on charges of soliciting.

Poor girls, they probably find the interiors of the Thirty Thousand Courts even more dark, dreary and dismal than the squalid rooms in which they provide sex for a few hundred rupees a session, and the establishment often doesn't come to their aid when they're in trouble. They have to scout around for assistance, and touts like Bihari accost them to help them and exploit them alike, while, their hands tied with a rope that substitutes for handcuffs, they are being dragged by surly-looking policemen to the Magistrate's court.

So the story is that some of these women tell the lawyers who are helping them get bail that they don't have the money right now, and please could they pay in kind? And then the girls tell the madams in the establishment, who see nothing wrong in offering some kind of a discount. You'll notice that in some of the lawyers' chambers on the criminal side there is a kind of staircase leading up to a small attic just above their office where they relax with these ladies. Most of the women who travel up these staircases are hookers, their lawyers (who now happen to be their clients, in a curious reversal of relationships) breathlessly climbing up the stairs behind them. There may be some who are clients, women who need representation, or women who need representation for their brothers and husbands who are likewise told to pay in kind. Yes, Lord Patel, it's a sordid kind of sex that takes place in those chambers, and sometimes a lawyer allows some of his younger colleagues, or even juniors assisting him, to also use the prostitute's services.

I assure you that never have I, in all these years that I have been in the Thirty Thousand Courts, ever been tempted even remotely by the idea of climbing up the stairs with a young exploited woman. Of course, I have been lucky enough to have had a few normal, ordinary relationships with respectable women, including a couple of rather special long-term relationships too. I don't need to pay for sex.

Why do I laugh, you ask? I'm sorry to have spluttered over my drink. I'm afraid some drops of whisky may have soiled the front of your Louis Vuitton shirt. No matter, you say. That's very kind of you. I'm truly sorry, Lord Patel, I truly am. But you're right. The laughter came to me suddenly while I still had the whisky in my mouth, so I choked momentarily and spluttered.

I was laughing because it suddenly occurred to me that you and I, for all our differences, have two things in common.

One is that both of us know how to conduct ourselves successfully in different situations. You, sir, know how to deal directly with the workers in one of your factories operating a lathe machine, or so I've read. You understand where they are coming from because to some extent – not comparable of course, but you know what I mean, to some extent – you too have had a deprived childhood. You have therefore sat with the high and the low.

And the same goes for me too. By a curious chance, I obtained membership of New Delhi's famous Sports Club – a club, by the way, that even many of the wealthiest residents of this city cannot get access to. But I'm a member and I go there every second weekend to play bridge, swim in the pool and drink whisky in the Board Room. But I also drink at Johnny's, frequented by common criminals and low-ranking policemen. So you and I have both moved in different societies, but, whereas you have left the 'down-and-out' part of your former existence, I still move between the lowest and the highest. But what made me laugh at that instant was the realisation that sitting with you today in Johnny's bar was a different kind of situation. I have dined and drunk with paupers in bars such as the present one, and I have drunk and dined with those belonging to the uppermost strata of society in five-star hotel bars and places like the Board Room, but this – and it was this that made me laugh – this is the first time I have been drinking and dining with a prince such as you undoubtedly are. Don't shake your head, dear sir – it's not the title that's important, but you know perfectly well what I mean. This is the first time I have dined and drunk with a prince in places such as Nathu's and Johnny's.

And the second thing we have in common, Lord Patel, is that for both of us there is one person whom we love above all others. You were widowed some years ago, Lord Patel, and although you have remarried I can deduce that you love your son more than you love your second wife – she is more in the nature of a trophy that a rich man picks up somewhere along the climb up the Fortune 500 List – or indeed any other human being; and for me, as you might guess, with my unmarried status and with both my parents deceased, my sister was the most important person in my life.

Why do the tears spring to my eyes just now? It's because, when I said she was the most important person in my life, it came to me once again that she is no more, that she died some months ago, while I held her in my arms and she sobbed her heart out at what your son and his friend had done to her.

Let me pour myself another drink and then I will tell you what happened to my sister. And also what happened to your son. Isn't that the reason why you've come to see me, accepting all my conditions, and have accompanied me through the hot dusty streets, to have lunch and then to sit next to me in this bar?

I will tell you about my sister first, about the fateful day when she went to Jhilmil Lake with your son and his friend, and after that I suggest that you too have a drink. For you will need it in order to hear what followed.

* * *

You're wondering why I've brought you to this unlicensed bar. Am I in a mood to get drunk tonight? Yes, I am – and, although you say you don't want to join me for a drink, after you hear what I'm now about to tell you I believe that you will change your mind.

Do you know why we like to have bars like this so close to the lowly lower courts in the capital? Of course it's good business, but we need these places because sometimes we badly crave a drink, the policemen and lawyers alike. You see, Lord Patel, we observe so many horrible things, we do so many terrible things, that often after work we need to be able to rush off into some bar where we can forget what we've seen, what we've done. It's why these places exist.

Kumar Jain, our client, was in a blue funk, as the expression goes, when he arrived at my chambers with a copy of the summons and the petition that Singhania and Kapoor had filed on behalf of your son, seeking restitution of the property. Amit filed the case for restitution immediately after returning to Delhi from Bombay. Singhania and Kapoor pulled out all the stops. They hurried to the court of the Rent Controller, alleging fraud and demanding immediate restitution of the premises.

I gave Kumar Jain some cool water to drink from the *surahi* you've seen in my chambers and asked him to calm down. I called Bihari immediately. After fifteen minutes he dropped by. It was late afternoon and he suggested that we all walk across to one of these unlicensed bars to discuss the situation properly. Once we had drunk a couple of beers each, and outlined our future stratagem to Kumar Jain, the poor fellow began to breathe more easily. And we all began to laugh.

You see, Lord Patel, after we had evicted your son from the White House, the place was lying empty. Mr Jain himself had not had time to move back in. That, as it turned out, was a stroke of good luck for us. Singhania and Kapoor's reputation was at stake. When a client engages a big law firm, he pays for the work they do on his behalf, but also for the clout that they command. The partners at Singhania and Kapoor know many of the Supreme Court and High Court justices on a first-name basis, and they turned all the levers they could to assure them a fast-track restitution of the White House property, alleging fraud on the part of Kumar Jain, my client. Amit demanded immediate restitution of his tenancy rights in the White House, and he could well have been successful if he'd been seeking it from Kumar Jain.

Legally speaking, the only way we could block this was to argue that Kumar Jain had already let out the premises to a third party, who had rented it in good faith soon after the eviction had taken place. All we needed to produce was a fake tenant, one of Kumar Jain's umpteen business buddies, someone who would come to court, and demand to be made a party to the proceedings on the ground that he had taken the property on lease in good faith from Kumar Jain, upon finding it unoccupied. This man, this fake tenant, a trusted man who would be in cahoots with us, would produce before the court a backdated lease agreement, signed by Kumar Jain and the fake tenant, duly recorded and attested by a Notary Public, within days after the eviction. He would also need to demonstrate physical possession of the property.

Not so easy to get a fake attestation, you think? Easiest thing in the world. And that's why we laughed so hard that afternoon as we sipped our cold beers.

You see, Lord Patel, in hundreds of courts across the country, immediately outside the court building, under thatched roofs, tarpaulins or blue skies, you'll find men sitting at small tables selling stamp paper. You'll also find the officials who will attest those stamped documents after they have been typed up – commonly designated as Notaries Public and Oath Commissioners.

I don't have to tell you, Lord Patel – a Harvard law graduate – how indelibly stamps and stamping are connected in the public mind with legality. And not without reason. All those property agreements that your son signed off on, the powers of attorney, the agreements to sell, the affidavits – all those documents need to be executed on stamp paper and often require attestation or authentication, don't they?

So far so good, but how does the system operate in real life in India? Let us assume that you yourself are a first-time visitor to the Thirty Thousand Courts. You've come to prepare an affidavit – an affidavit that states that your son has been found, and you no longer wish to press any charges against me. You'd be more than happy to do that, you say. Well, let's leave that particular discussion aside for the time being.

You've joined the small crowd collected near the stamp vendor's table, purchased the stamp paper for the required amount, have got your statement typed up and now you wish to have it attested.

As you wander through the Thirty Thousand Courts complex in search of a suitable attestator, you will see scores of boards which state how various documents can be attested. The Oath Commissioner and Notary Public seem omnipresent, like policemen on Delhi roads these days.

An observant man like you will immediately notice something strange. The same name – for example, M. P. Sharma – will crop up again and again. Clearly, since it's your first time, you'll be confused as to how so many M. P. Sharmas can exist – even though this is not unimaginable considering that there are four-thousand-odd members of the Bar. The fact of the matter, however, is that there may be only one Mr M. P. Sharma, Notary Public.

Sharma-ji has managed to gain custody of several tables or 'seats' all over the *kacheri* at strategic points, such as near the courts complex entrances, where maximum business can be procured. His tables are manned by touts and their assistants, who all receive a commission. That's how it works.

For the authentication system to operate properly, you should find the Notary Public at his table. You should be sitting face to face when he puts his seal and signs off. But you will not find them there. Mr Sharma himself may possibly be lounging in one of the innumerable court canteens with his friends, discussing perhaps a recent altercation between a lawyer and a judge. The touts or their assistants run from these tables to the cafeteria with the affidavits, lease agreements, powers of attorney, whatever these documents might be, telling the clients at the tables to hang on. In the café M. P. Sharma signs them breezily, jotting the details down in a notebook so he can keep track of the number of documents attested and the amounts charged – for the settlement of accounts in the evening.

You sigh. How is any of this relevant, you ask yourself. I'm just painting a picture – for your knowledge and understanding – and providing general background to explain why there are so many fake documents being passed around and accepted as real. To say that what happens is a violation of the law is not saying much, because this is only the tip of the proverbial iceberg. There exist far grosser transgressions of the law and malpractices.

Mr M. P. Sharma, the gentleman of whom we spoke, being a lawyer as well as a Notary Public, would not want to be seen directly setting up so many stalls all around the court complex. He gets someone like Bihari to oversee and co-ordinate the whole affair. As a matter of fact, Bihari does oversee the functioning of five or six tables, and therefore for us there is nothing even remotely challenging about procuring backdated stamp papers and attestations.

As we ordered another round of beer, Kumar Jain telephoned a business associate, a small shopkeeper from the crowded quarter of Old Delhi, who had agreed to be our dummy tenant for the White House in Golf Links. An hour later he came over to my chamber, to which Bihari, Kumar Jain and I had returned. The four of us wandered across to one of the stamp vendors, then to the typist's block to get the material typed, and then finally we produced the attestation.

Ten thousand rupees stuffed into the Notary Public's coat pocket, two thousand rupees pressed into the stamp vendor's palm. That's all it took.

All in a day's work, as the expression goes. We now had a nicely legal-looking document to throw in the face of the representatives of Singhania and Kapoor, who had got the very next day fixed for hearing the matter –

an urgent short-notice date they had managed to obtain from the Registrar, bribing him no doubt with some 'speed money' as well as using their considerable clout.

When the case came up for hearing the following day, the judge stared at the lease agreement between Kumar Jain and Satish Jain, the fake tenant we had produced in court, and was satisfied, after examining the date on which the stamp paper had been issued as well as the notarial stamp dates, that the document was genuine. He handed it over to Singhania and Kapoor's Harvard-trained lawyers to examine and find fault with. The two youngsters looked at it carefully and turned it around, but they couldn't find anything wrong, for it had been casually but meticulously prepared.

At this stage the dummy tenant's lawyer – Mr Tomar, the colleague next door, who had been properly briefed by me – ventured to give the judge a copy of a recent Supreme Court judgement, which ruled that bona fide third parties who rented a property should not be penalised or evicted for no fault of their own, even if there was some evidence of underhand dealing in securing the eviction of the previous tenant. The judge brushed it aside, telling him that he was already aware of it, and told Singhania and Kapoor that his hands were tied in the light of Supreme Court rulings, and no urgent orders for restitution of possession could be passed in such a case even if, for the sake of argument, it was accepted that there existed some proof or evidence of fraud.

Your son, Lord Patel, hadn't turned up in court with his lawyers, and this confirmed to me once again that he was guilty of what I suspected him of doing and could not bring himself to face me in court. It also told me that he had taken my threats seriously.

17

Property prices in India are on a par with real estate prices in the most expensive parts of the world. Don't you agree, Lord Patel? A two-bedroom apartment in certain parts of Delhi or Bombay is as expensive as a property in Manhattan, New York, and comparable in price to those in the most expensive areas of London.

And so, as part of this property-buying spree, your son decided to go down to Jhilmil Lake to see the possibility of an acquisition there. In this regard, Lord Patel, I believe that Amit was influenced by you – isn't that so? Just as Nathu's son was influenced by his father's idea that if you keep the quality of your products high the customer will return to you again and again.

Early on in life you yourself learned that acquisition was the way forward. I remember reading an interview with you some time ago, Lord Patel, in which you said that, had you stuck to 'developing' an industry or setting up new industries from scratch, you could never have made the headway you did. The secret of the rapid growth of your copper companies lay in your relentless pursuit of the acquisition of companies that other people had set up, when these people were keen to get rid of the businesses because they were making losses. You brought your understanding of the copper business and sound management principles to these failed institutions and turned them around into profit-making enterprises within the space of a year or so. See, even I understand some business.

You started with copper – such an important commodity after all. The *Wall Street Journal* had a write-up about your company only last week. And while, in this age of rising oil prices, share prices have taken a tumble in markets across the globe, not so with your company. You worked very hard building up an empire, then once you became the acknowledged King of Copper, following your acquisition of a large Swedish company with major interests across Africa, you decided to diversify and went into the real estate business. It was like the rest of your ideas: absolutely brilliant and perfectly timed. The slump in property prices in the US following the sub-prime mortgage crisis, the slump in property prices in London and the booming property market in Asia created a situation where a lot of money could be made by an intelligent investor. And so you decided to set up your son Amit in the international real estate business. You yourself would continue to focus on and control the copper empire, but now and again you would give your son a word of encouragement and advice, if you felt it was needed. You were interested in the whole of Asia, with property prices shooting up in Singapore, Thailand and Malaysia, but India was of special interest, not only because of your ancestral connections but because the market here was especially lucrative. And so you set up Patel Holdings and Properties, Asia, with your headquarters in New Delhi.

But, Lord Patel, I can see that you look tired now. Perhaps it is time now to come to the end of our story . . . ah, the so very sad ending to this tale. I believe that I now possess a measure of equanimity about what happened to my beloved sister – although I will never recover from the horrific and tragic loss – since it was two days short of a year ago that she expired in my arms.

You look disturbed. You share in my sorrow, perhaps, for you too have been so anxious on account of a loved one these past few months. It has been a year since my sister died, but it has been only six months since the day your son disappeared.

Didn't you come to see me, Lord Patel, because you believe that I am the only person in the world who can tell you whether your son is alive or not? Is this not the case? You nod sorrowfully, almost pleadingly. Don't embarrass me any further, I beg of you.

Come, let's end this tale. I'll take you to your son now. Yes, Lord Patel, right now. Let's be done with this place. I assure you, dear sir, we'll be with him in less than ten minutes. We're going to see your son, and it's an occasion to celebrate, isn't it?

I've finished my drink, but my throat is still a trifle parched. Shall we have one last drink? One for the road? Mistri-ji, can we have one more large peg of Scotch? Yes, I mean one peg for each of us, Mistri-ji. Of course, my friend will keep me company.

I'm done, Lord Patel. If you drink up, we can go. No, please do finish your whisky. I can wait. We cannot waste perfectly good Scotch, in these times, what with the food crisis and spiralling oil prices. And whisky, too, is a kind of oil. Oil for troubled souls. Like yours and mine, Lord Patel. You laugh. I can see your spirits have lifted at the thought that you will soon be with your son.

You've finished? Good, good. Let's go at once. I can't bear to hear these sad songs any more. Let's walk to my chambers. Yes, to my chambers, I said. It's there that you will meet your son. He's waiting for us. Come, let's go. And on the way I'll tell you how I happened to lose my sister.

Lord Patel, I'm so glad that you came today without the tall, muscular, armed bodyguards that usually accompany you. Of course it was one of the conditions that I had laid down for this meeting, that you should come unaccompanied. It must have been a while since you've driven a car in India yourself – but it's one of those things that you never forget. I hope we don't have any security people waiting on the streets outside. You assure me that that's not the case. Well, I certainly do take you for a man of your word, Lord Patel.

Part Nine
A Last Supper?

18

Now that we've had our drinks, I want to explain how I came to suspect that Amit and Sunil had laid a trap for Ruhno. The fact that she was such a virtuous girl made them only more desperate. It wasn't very difficult for them to hatch a plan, for she had started doing this consultancy work for them, going off to sites to see properties and to examine the financial implications of any investments. It wasn't something she had any special expertise in, and that made me suspicious of Sunil and Amit's intentions, but she just dismissed all my objections. My sister was a grown-up woman, and I couldn't insist that she take heed of my advice and steer clear of these two characters beyond a certain point. The problem was, of course, that she was in love with Amit, and that's why she rebelled against me, if I might call it that.

Anyhow, she had this new car, a Maruti, that she had bought with a bank loan, the way everyone buys vehicles these days, and she was driving to college and to different property sites within Delhi as part of her consultancy work with Patel Properties and Holdings. Sometimes she went with Amit, sometimes with Amit and Sunil, and sometimes with some other staff member. She generally kept me informed of all her travels, and I wasn't too worried, because I thought I had alerted her as to Amit and Sunil's possible intentions towards her, and I was sure she could take care of herself.

Most days she came home earlier than I did. She still prepared dinner for me, even though I told her several times that with her additional duties in college and with the consultancy work we should get hold of a cook. No, she insisted, we may have our disagreements over what kind of a person Amit is, but I still love you more than anyone else in the world, and I don't want to see anyone else preparing your meals just so long as we are together. Did she think that Amit was going to propose marriage to her and that she would soon be gone? I really don't know.

Some days she was late because there was an evening function at the college or because she was going out to a movie with some friend from college, and occasionally she went out for dinner with Amit. Over time my anxieties became less though they did not disappear.

One morning over breakfast she told me that after college she was going to Jhilmil Lake with Amit and Sunil, to survey some land there that Patel Properties was interested in acquiring. There would be a meeting with the seller, followed by dinner and discussion, and she would be late coming back. I told her that her evening's programme was well timed and suited me fine because I myself had been invited to my friend Prem Sharma's house for a small party with close friends, to celebrate his daughter's engagement a few days earlier – the daughter who in Prem Sharma's own words had been trained by her mother, his wife, in how to 'keep men on a leash'. Prem was fond of drinking and revelry (much to his wife's dislike), and so it was likely to be a late-night affair. I would probably reach home later than Ruhno.

Prem's apartment was only a few blocks away from mine. We were getting together after a longer than usual interval, and he kept refilling my glass, insisting that I have 'just one more for the road' and pointing out how it would take me less than five minutes to drive home. It was nearly one in the morning, later than usual, and when I saw his wife give him a few warning looks, to which he himself was oblivious, I decided it was time to call it a day, or rather night.

As my old Fiat approached my house I saw the lights were on in the apartment, which meant that Ruhno was home and waiting for me. I parked the car outside on the main street, not far from her red Maruti, which she had driven into the garage. As I've explained to you, Lord Patel, we live in a high-rise apartment in Mukerjee Nagar, on the third floor to be precise, and we also have allotted to us a small garage on the ground floor. Earlier, I used to park my Fiat inside this garage, but when Ruhno bought her new Maruti we decided that her car should go inside and mine could be parked outside in the open.

The garage was open, but that in itself was not surprising, since the steel shutter was rusty and sometimes Ruhno had a problem pulling it down. But I saw something red glowing inside. Has she left the engine on, I wondered. The light was of a different kind and spread though the garage, and I couldn't hear the sound of the engine. I stepped out of the Fiat, walked across to the Maruti and tried to look inside but it was all dark except for the red glow. And then when I switched on the light I made out the shape of a body slumped against the window on the other side towards the driver's seat. I hurried around the car and peered inside again, and shock waves ripped through my body. It was my darling Ruhno. I tried to open the door then, but all the doors had been locked from the inside. I normally carry the spare key to the Maruti in my pocket, as sometimes I use her car for short trips to the nearby grocery store or to the whisky shop. Trembling with fear, I searched in my pocket for the key, but realised that by chance I had left it in the apartment – on this occasion, where every minute was precious. Panic-stricken, and desperate not to lose any time, I looked around, spotted a large brick left by some kid playing a game in the corner, picked it up, and brought it down with all my force on the window of the front passenger door. The glass shattered. I put my hand in and opened the car door from the passenger's side. Smoke rushed out, temporarily choking me. The car was full of smoke and fumes and the red glow was that of her portable charcoal stove, which had been left burning on the dashboard.

The smoke became less dense, allowing me to grab the still smouldering charcoal stove with my handkerchief and throw it outside against the pavement.

I climbed inside the car and shook her savagely, crying out her name again and again. Her eyes flickered open briefly. I saw in them a brief light of recognition. She put her head on my shoulder then, and uttered a few choking sobs.

'Why did you do this?' I shouted hoarsely, pulling her face towards mine.

'I was raped, *bhaiya*,' she said in a dull voice, and then repeated the same words. 'I was raped.'

Before I could ask any further question, she saw it in my eyes and said, 'Sunil Gupta. It was Sunil.'

'And Amit?' I shouted, close to tears myself.

'I don't know,' she moaned, and then she asked for something to drink. 'Coffee!' she moaned, started to cough, and then slumped to the other side once more.

I starting shaking her again but she didn't respond. I looked around for help but there was no one about. Not realising how late it was, I formed the irrational and angry notion that here was my beloved sister suffocating to death, yet nobody in the neighbourhood had even noticed, not even my nosy neighbour, Mrs Ahuja.

Broken glass from the window had fallen on the seat, and I pushed it outside. Then I opened the driver's door from the inside, slipped out of the car, and came in again from the driver's side. I pushed Ruhno over to the passenger seat and turned the key that was still in the ignition, hoping the car would start. It sprang to life immediately. The car was working. Thank God for that. I would have lost a few minutes trying to transfer her body, now grown limp, to my Fiat, which was parked just outside the garage. Besides, the Maruti was new, had rapid acceleration and would reach the hospital faster.

When we reached Kirori Mal Hospital, just a fifteen-minute drive away, I was hopeful of her recovery. The staff there didn't waste any time in getting her medical attention. There was a pink-faced, paunchy policeman stationed just near Emergency, as is usually the case. Sometimes these fellows insist on getting their register filled up in accident cases, before they allow any of the accident victims to receive medical attention, for they deem them to be medico-legal cases – while the patient is dying, can you imagine this? – but here there was no bleeding and no broken bones, so he let us through without much delay.

The nurses wheeled Ruhno into the Intensive Care Unit and within moments she was on a white bed, where the nurses were putting tubes into her body. Someone shouted for an oxygen cylinder. It arrived within a few minutes, while I stood waiting, my heart screaming with anxiety, and then they attached a tube to it and put the other end in through her mouth towards her windpipe. There was no high-pressure oxygen room in the hospital, and this was the best they could do.

They took out some blood then, which I learned later was to estimate the extent to which her haemoglobin had combined with the carbon monoxide. It was a bright-red colour, brighter than normal, and I was told that the brighter it was the worse the situation. The doctor said that when up to sixty per cent of the haemoglobin had combined with the carbon monoxide there were chances of survival, but here it was eighty per cent. There was very little chance that she would live. They tried all they could, but she never regained consciousness.

Yes, they tried everything, but they couldn't save her. There is a five-star hospital in South Delhi with a fully oxygenated room, and had I taken her to that hospital there would have been a possibility, albeit remote, that she might have survived. There was, however, simply no way I could have covered the distance from our house in Mukerjee Nagar to the five-star hospital in time. I had taken the right decision by bringing her to the nearest hospital, but it was too late. The smoke had penetrated her lungs completely.

The day my sister died, there were only two days left until her twenty-third birthday. Just that evening, before going to the party at Prem's house, I had walked across to Miranda's Pastry Shop, our favourite bakery since Ruhno was a small girl, and had, ironically enough, placed an order for 'Death by Chocolate', a dark, extremely rich chocolate cake with chocolate icing, which I knew she would love – chocolate cakes were her favourite dessert.

Someone in the hospital must have alerted the duty police constable, the pink-faced paunchy man who had let us pass, that there had been a death under what could be termed 'unnatural circumstances', for soon after the doctor had told me that Ruhno had died, and I was paying the bill and making arrangements for an ambulance to bring the body home and carry it upstairs on a stretcher to my apartment on the third floor, the fellow arrived with a grey-haired, sad-faced sub-inspector, who looked as if he had just been woken up.

'How did this happen?' the inspector asked me.

'She forgot to close the cooking gas,' I said. 'I'm her brother. I reached home late, and found her unconscious in the bedroom.'

'Was it suicide, do you think?' he said, in the manner of someone asking a routine question.

'Definitely not,' I said.

'Was there any note left behind by her?' he persisted.

'No,' I said.

'Did you notice if she was upset about anything in particular over the last few days?' he asked yet again.

'No,' I said, sharply this time. I was not going to answer any more questions. 'I've told you. It was an accident.'

'All right,' he said, his deadpan expression changing into one of deep sympathy. I guess he had seen enough deaths to know that this wasn't a case of fratricide. Besides, in India, if you want to kill off a female member of your family, you use the kerosene-stove method – a saree catches fire while she was supposedly cooking a meal – and charcoal stove suicides inside a car are relatively unknown. I understand, though, that they are not so uncommon in Japan, where coincidentally the stove was manufactured.

The sub-inspector was saying, 'I know this is difficult for you, but I need you to wait a while, answer a few more questions and sign a statement.

I'll need to record a finding based on your statement that there is no reason to suspect either foul play or suicide.' He grimaced. 'Otherwise, they'll have to do a full autopsy and cut her up.' He pursed his lips sympathetically. 'I'm sorry about this.'

He pointed to a desk with three chairs, kept in a corner, possibly for this purpose alone. 'Let's go there.'

We went and sat down. The inspector took out various forms and filled them in. There were some more routine questions and, as he had promised, in ten minutes it was over. Meanwhile, a nurse came along with the death certificate, and she said the ambulance was ready and waiting to take Ruhno home.

I brought her body home, the ambulance following my car. They didn't ask me about the smashed front glass, assuming possibly that in my hurry to the hospital I had hit something. Or someone. Anyhow, they didn't ask anything. I called my close friends, my *maasi* – my late mother's sister – and the neighbours. Prem Sharma and Ashok Kumar, another friend from Uni, turned up with their wives, and the neighbours arrived; my *maasi* and her husband came, and she took out a family address book from her handbag and made phone calls to our relatives. The women took charge, washing Ruhno, dressing her body in a bright-red saree; they said there would be no white for someone as young as she was. I sat in a corner, not talking to anyone. Lost to the world. But inside I was seething, thinking and plotting.

The English have a saying, don't they, Lord Patel, that revenge is a dish best served cold. I never understood the meaning of that phrase until the day Ruhno died.

19

Here we are at my chambers, Lord Patel. Hetram will have gone home a while ago. It's all deserted here at this time, unlike the chambers in the criminal wing, where there will still be some lawyers sitting in their offices with a drink, enjoying the cool evening. Let me open the door, and switch on the light.

Yes, please come in and have a seat. You know, Lord Patel, I've invited you here today of all days in the year for a special reason. I could also have called you two days earlier, which would have been the first anniversary of my sister's death, but I chose to invite you today instead because she died just two days before her birthday. Today she would have turned twenty-four.

I asked Hetram to fetch a small chocolate cake called 'Death by Chocolate', which my sister would have loved, similar to the one I bought for her just over a year ago. I want to have a slice in her memory. Let me see if he has put it in this small cupboard. Yes, it is here! I see that he has left it alongside a half-bottle of Vat 69 Scotch whisky. Post-liberalisation, all such good things are freely available in shops across the country.

Let me take out the cake first and place it on the table. Ah, there are a few candles here as well. Good fellow, Hetram. He did not forget. Let me put just one candle on top. I have a matchbox. Now we will light it. There, it is lit. Let's wait for it to go out on its own before eating the cake. And meanwhile let me pour both of us a shot of Scotch whisky – what do you say, Lord Patel? Shall I give us a double measure? Yes. Very good. Here you are, sir.

The day after my sister's death I drove to Jhilmil Lake, straight from the cremation ground. I had taken the Maruti to the garage early that morning, as I didn't want people in the neighbourhood asking too many questions.

Of course, with relatives and friends who soon began pouring into my apartment to offer their condolences, questions were inevitable. How had Ruhno suffocated to death? I had to tell them all that it had been an accidental death, she had left the gas on and suffocated to death; I didn't want more people than necessary asking questions. There was another reason why I wanted the smashed front window to be replaced and the interior fumigated and cleaned. In some way I wanted to pretend to myself that, while it was true that Ruhno was no longer alive, the previous night's episode had never occurred. I wanted to pretend to myself that she had died in an accident. I wanted to remember her smiling, happy face, you see, not the sobbing, tormented woman who had given up her life for nothing.

The garage owner was a friend, who had serviced my old Fiat for decades and had been telling me to get a new vehicle for a long time. The news about Ruhno's death had still not reached him, so he was his usual cheerful self. He promised to get a new window installed and have the car delivered to me before noon. So the Maruti was back in the garage by the time the Pandit had performed the *havan* and finished the discourse on the *Bhagavad Gita*. Ruhno's body had been washed by my *chachi*, with Mrs Ahuja helping, and had been dressed in a bright-red saree, one of her favourites, as befitted a young, unmarried woman.

As I turned from Faridabad Modh towards Jhilmil Lake, I could still smell in the car the faint whiff of the perfume that she used; neither the smoke nor the subsequent fumigation had destroyed the fragrance completely. What had Sunil Gupta done to my beloved sister? I needed to find out if there was anyone who would tell me what had happened and – what was equally important – if there was anyone who would testify against Sunil Gupta. You see, Lord Patel, at that time I wasn't sure about the extent or nature of your son's involvement in the affair, for Ruhno had told me that it was Sunil Gupta who had raped her. Your son's name wasn't mentioned at all, but then she hadn't had time to talk.

Jhilmil Lake, while situated in the neighbouring state of Haryana, is a popular weekend getaway for Delhiites. While you are likely to see families there as well, it's especially popular with young romancing couples. As the name suggests, it has a large lake in the centre. When Ruhno had mentioned to me her planned trip to the area, stating that negotiations were afoot between Patel Holdings and Properties and the Government of Haryana, I didn't smell anything suspicious, because as you know, Lord Patel, these days everything is getting privatised. I had reflected upon the loss to hundreds of poor hapless couples who would now have to travel further away to find a place where they could enjoy privacy. It did cross my mind that it might also be a pleasure trip disguised as business, and perhaps it was only a short romantic trip undertaken by Amit and Ruhno. But there too I had already voiced my concerns, and had even met you, and I thought that I had thereby effectively blocked any troubles my sister could face. She had been most embarrassed by my visit to you, so I wasn't going to raise the issue with her again.

I parked the Maruti next to a large building that you reach soon after passing a big signboard advertising the delights of Jhilmil Lake, just outside the main entrance. I got out of the car, walked through the entrance, saw the reception building and strolled across to make enquiries. I noticed that there was a board showing vacancies.

At reception I was met by a young, friendly South Indian, who introduced himself as Rangarajan, the manager of the establishment. The story I told him was that a relative of mine, a young woman, had visited Jhilmil Lake the previous day together with Sunil Gupta and Amit Patel, and had not yet returned home. As she was a relatively young person, I had been asked by her elderly parents to investigate the matter before contacting the police. I took out a photo of Ruhno and showed it to him.

'I haven't seen her.' He shook his head. 'I know Sunil Gupta, though. He is a regular client of ours, since the days when he worked with Dhoom Television. I understand he is now with Patel Holdings and Properties, and I believe that Amit Patel has visited Jhilmil Lake, but I myself haven't had the opportunity to meet him.' He scratched his head. 'Excuse me, sir, but don't her parents have any idea of her whereabouts?'

'No, they don't,' I said. 'I've already spoken to them, and neither of them has any idea, because she came here in her own car.'

Rangarajan looked sympathetic, but said that he didn't think he could help in any way. 'If you leave the photo with me, I can check with some of the staff.'

'Let that be for the time being,' I said, carefully studying his expression, 'because this is the only photo I have. I'll wander about your place and make my own enquiries. By the way, have you heard of any proposal for Jhilmil Lake to be sold to a private party?'

'No, I haven't.' He raised his eyebrows. 'I would be extremely surprised if that happened. We're doing very well, sir.' He shook his head sceptically. 'It's possible, of course, but why would the Government want to sell an establishment that was doing so well, and earning so much revenue?'

'That's true,' I said. 'Can you tell me if Mr Sunil Gupta had a booking for any of these rooms here?'

'Certainly, sir.' He quickly flipped through the pages of a register. 'Ah, here it is. He was booked into Cottage 16, for two nights only. We have thirty rooms in this main building for visitors who want to stay overnight and we also have about thirty cottages all around the lake – those are more expensive.'

'Two nights, did you say?' I asked him.

'Yes, sir,' he replied. 'He checked out yesterday morning.'

'Did he personally check out?'

'No, sir,' he responded. 'Mr Gupta is one of our regular customers and there has never been any problem about payment. He leaves whenever he likes, handing the keys to the attendant. There is an attendant in each cottage.' He paused. 'Would you like me to call the attendant of Cottage 16 here, so you can talk to him?'

'No, don't bother,' I said, not wanting to give the attendant any time to prepare his responses while he walked from the cottage to reception. 'I'll just walk across and talk to him if he's there. Will he be there?'

'Oh yes, sir,' he said. He looked at another register. 'And it's the same person who was on duty that day, sir. His name is Ranvir Singh.'

I left the reception area. A brisk fifteen-minute walk took me to Cottage 16. It was locked and the attendant was nowhere to be seen, but the lake was just opposite. Rather than wait for the attendant, I decided to stroll down to the lake and return later. There were small boats bobbing up and down, some with romancing couples and others with families including two or three of their offspring.

A large building next to the lake had a signboard that read 'Copa Cabana'. I saw tables inside and waiters in white uniforms. It was a restaurant. I entered and took a window table overlooking the lake. A young lad, who must have been thirteen or fourteen, approached my table with a menu card. He looked like someone born in the northern hills. I asked him where he came from, and by a coincidence he was from Himachal Pradesh, from a small village not far from Shimla. I spoke to him using fragments of the mountain dialect that I had picked up during my visits to that state, and I thought he seemed well pleased.

I ordered a pot of tea, and when the boy returned with the tea I asked him if he knew where Ranvir Singh, the attendant of Cottage 16, was to be found. Apparently he was in the cafeteria gossiping with one of the security guards. The boy said he would bring him over.

As I waited for Ranvir Singh, I poured myself a cup of tea and gazed out across the lake. You will appreciate, Lord Patel, how disturbing I found it to be at the place where my sister had spent the day before with your son. I thought of how she would possibly have gone on a boat trip with Amit only the previous day, and wondered if she had remembered Shimla as the boat drifted over the waters of this lake surrounded by hills on all sides. Then I found myself thinking of Shimla and all the places I had visited there with Ruhno.

A tall, pock-marked fellow in khaki was standing near my table with the young boy.

'My name is Ranvir Singh, *sa'ab*,' he said. 'This young lad says you want to speak to me.'

'Yes,' I said, and I took out Ruhno's photograph and showed it to him. 'Have you seen this lady?'

'Yes, sir,' he said. 'She was here yesterday with Mr Amit, in Cottage 16.'

'Well, she is missing now,' I said. 'Do you know when Mr Amit left?'

'No, sir,' he replied. 'They came together, and I asked if they needed anything. They told me they didn't, and they'd walk across to the cafeteria and order it if they did need anything. I'm in charge of two more cottages, 17 and 18, and I got busy over there then. By the time I got back, they had left.'

'Do you have any idea if they left together or when they left?'

'No, I don't,' he replied.

I was trying to keep my feelings in check, but my expression would doubtless have betrayed my deep distress. This man standing in front of me was clearly worried, and he was trying to say as little as possible to me, for fear of making a mistake.

I said, 'Reception told me the cottage was booked in Sunil Gupta's name.'

'That's right, sir,' he replied. 'Mr Gupta sometimes does the booking in his own name but gives the keys to his friends. He has done that in the past, so I didn't think anything of it.'

'Did you see Sunil Gupta yesterday?' I asked, watching him very carefully.

There was the barest flicker of hesitation, but it was there, and I saw it.

'I did not see him, sir.'

'Well, all right then,' I said, dismissively. 'That will be all.'

I watched him go, rage smouldering inside me. I poured myself another cup of tea, and asked the lad, who was still standing there, to fetch me a single cigarette of the best imported brand he could find. He darted off, and returned with a Benson & Hedges. I hadn't smoked a cigarette for many years, and didn't have a light, so he went off again to get a box of matches, came back and struck a match for me, anxious to please.

Did I want anything to eat, he asked.

'No,' I said, 'but I want to ask you about a man who visited this cafeteria yesterday, and the more you tell me about him, the more money it will be worth to you.' Then I placed a 500-rupee note on the table. I cast an eye over the cafeteria to check that Ranvir Singh was not hanging about in the vicinity. 'This man,' I added, 'is tall, with a big build, and wears a jet-black wig. It's easy to make out that it's a wig.'

The boy looked round the cafeteria, and I knew then that he too was making sure that the cottage attendant was not there, and that he had something to tell me.

'Yes,' said the boy, 'this man was here, sitting at that table in the corner.' He pointed to a table at the other end of the cafeteria. 'He sat there for about forty-five minutes and had three cups of coffee. There wasn't much rush at that time of day, and I had nothing to do, so I decided to observe the man with the wig. All the while he kept looking at his watch. Finally, he ordered a double omelette, which I took to his table. As I was returning to the counter, I heard his mobile phone ring. I turned back and noticed he wasn't answering it but was looking at the screen as if to see who had called. After a few rings, the phone stopped ringing. The man summoned me to ask how much the bill was. I said I would get it made up and come back, but he said he didn't have time. He left a hundred rupees on the table. He told me he thought that would cover three coffees and an omelette and I could keep the rest. Then he left the omelette uneaten on the table and rushed out.'

I gave the 500-rupee note to the boy. He was a decent lad, and said it wasn't necessary, but I insisted.

'What happened next?' I said. 'Or was that the end of your encounter?'

'Well, you see, sir,' the boy continued, 'I saw the man hurry towards Cottage 16, just across from our cafeteria, and I took the omelette back to the kitchen. Then I went back to where the man had been sitting, to swab the table, and I noticed a bunch of keys had fallen to the floor. I took the keys and ran outside towards Cottage 16, but Ranvir Singh was standing outside the cottage and blocked my entry, asking me my business. I explained that the tall fat man with the wig had left his keys in the cafeteria, and showed them to him. He grabbed them from me and told me to scram. He said he would personally give them to the gentleman.'

'I see. And then you returned to the cafeteria?'

'No. Something else happened. I heard a woman screaming. Three times. It was terrifying. The sound was coming from inside Cottage 16, and I instinctively started to walk back towards the cottage, but Ranvir Singh stopped me again. He had a stern expression on his face. He said it was none of my business. I said, there is a woman in trouble inside and we should help her, and he replied that I would be in trouble if I didn't listen to him. He was in charge of the cottage, and there was absolutely nothing to worry about. I could see he was nervous, though, but I didn't want any trouble, so I just went away. He tried to give me a ten-rupee note and ordered me to keep my mouth shut about what I'd heard, but I refused the money and said I wouldn't talk. And I haven't told anyone about it, but it's been preying on my mind ever since, for surely there was a woman in trouble inside that cottage that day and we should have done something to help her.'

As I looked at his scared young face, Lord Patel, it was clear to me that he would never stand up in court as a witness. He would be browbeaten into submission long before that by the Ranvir Singhs and Sunil Guptas of the world. And, if they did not succeed, the long-drawn-out court procedures would wear him down.

What was I thinking? Even if there had been a dozen witnesses, none would have dared come forward.

After my interview with the boy from Himachal, I walked back to where the Maruti was parked. I pulled open the door, climbed in and looked in the glove compartment. Nothing special: a bottle of perfume, a comb and a box of tissues. And yet, at the familiar sight of Ruhno's ordinary possessions, I put my head against the steering wheel and sobbed my heart out.

Oh, Ruhno, my darling sister! What was the need? Even if something so terrible had happened.

20

After my visit to Jhilmil Lake, I was still not entirely certain exactly how Amit was involved, and accordingly what punishment he deserved. Did your son know that Sunil was going to rape Ruhno? He was working for Patel Holdings and Properties after all. Amit could have easily stopped him with a word, a signal that Ruhno was important to him. And yet, while this was clearly the case, I couldn't be absolutely sure that Amit was involved in what had happened. In her dying moments my dear sister had said nothing against Amit. But now it did appear that I'd been right in assuming earlier on that your son was just having a good time with my sister, and that marriage to Ruhno was the last thing on his mind.

That, by itself, was not such a terrible deed, I must admit. Perhaps, Lord Patel, in our younger days, many of us have been guilty of leading a girl round the bush, or perhaps, to be more accurate, into a bush. Girls too play around with the feelings of boys who become besotted with them. It was, however, an entirely different matter if Amit had actively colluded in the rape of my sister. That, sir, could not be forgiven. I needed to find this out for sure, but unfortunately in my haste to wreak vengeance on Sunil Gupta I had possibly killed the only person, apart from your son himself, who could tell me what had really happened that day.

Ah, the candle has gone out. Let me cut the cake now. There is only a plastic knife and two plastic forks, but they will have to do. Here you are, Lord Patel. It's not such a big piece. But you would prefer to have the one that I have cut for myself? Because it is smaller? Very well. Whatever you like. I can have a bigger piece, because I don't think that I'm going to have any dinner later.

What I needed to do was to get your son out of the White House, and it was a strange coincidence, as I've mentioned to you earlier, that Kumar Jain came to Bihari and myself for help. Once Amit had been evicted, and his personal possessions, furniture, carpets, and so on, stored in a godown, a warehouse, in Old Delhi, I knew that despite the fact that Patel Properties and Holdings had a large number of properties, it would take time for him to move into one of his own.

And I was right in my assumptions. Amit, like any good businessman, decided to wait a while to see if his lawyers could fulfil their promise of getting him restitution of the White House property, and my guess is that he simultaneously instructed his staff to find somewhere else for him to live. Meanwhile, he moved into a five-star hotel in New Delhi, the Hyatt Regency.

And it was from there that I needed to get him kidnapped. I called Khargosh.

'It's a kidnapping this time, not a killing,' I told him.

Once he had the details of the person who needed to be 'lifted', to use the jargon of his trade, Khargosh told me he would undertake a preliminary investigation and then give me an estimate of how much it would cost me.

He called me three days later.

'It's going to cost you much more, *Guruji*, than the previous assignment,' he said. 'This man is currently staying at the Hyatt Regency hotel. I had one of my gang members follow him from his office in Connaught Place to the hotel. He always travels with two heavily built characters in the back of his car. From their looks, they could be ex-Indian Army soldiers. I also believe they are armed. Once they've delivered him to the hotel, they take taxis back to where they live. The next morning, they drive to the hotel in an official car – maybe they work for some security company.'

'Money is not an issue, Khargosh,' I said, 'but if he always has these bodyguards around him, how are we going to catch him alone?'

'We'll have to snatch him while he is at the hotel,' responded Khargosh, 'but we haven't yet figured out how.' He paused. 'Do you have any ideas, *Guruji*?'

'Let me think for a minute,' I said. I'd been thinking over this issue for much of the previous night without any concrete plan emerging, and then when Khargosh asked me this question, after thirty seconds of pondering it came to me in a flash. Maya. Of course! Maya Richards was the answer.

You see, Lord Patel, after what happened to my sister, I realised that my initial uneasy feeling about Maya Richards, Amit's personal secretary, on the day I visited your son in the White House was based on the likelihood that he was having a relationship with her. Yes, Lord Patel, your son was screwing Maya Richards. That, and not her professional skills, was the main reason why he brought her along to work with him in Delhi. I was pretty sure he was paying her a fortune. She hadn't been in the house at the time when Bihari and I got the White House vacated, since she had travelled with Amit to Bombay.

And now she wasn't staying with him at the Hyatt. My guess was that she would certainly come to visit him in the evenings, after going home and freshening up.

'Did anyone report seeing a blonde woman visiting the hotel?' I asked him.

After a pause he said, 'Yes, one of my team reported seeing a woman arrive every evening around seven o'clock. He said she was blonde, English-looking, very elegant.'

'Do you have any girls in your team, Khargosh?'

He hesitated for a few seconds, and then he said, 'It can be arranged, *Guruji*. Tell me what has to be done.'

'She should appear reasonably polished, and be able to speak English, Khargosh,' I said. 'This is important.' I paused.

'*Guruji*, we have the kind of girl you speak of,' he said, a trifle impatiently. 'Please go ahead with what you were saying.'

'There is a blonde woman by the name of Maya Richards, who works in our friend's office and also happens to be one of his many girlfriends,' I said, speaking slowly, so that there was no possibility of any misunderstanding. 'Can you write down that name please? Maya Richards.'

'I've got that, *Guruji*,' he said.

'If she visits the hotel at seven o'clock,' I pointed out, 'you need to arrive earlier, and you must lure Amit away an hour before she is due.'

'At six o'clock then, *Guruji*?'

'Yes, that should be okay. Now your girl has to go to Reception,' I continued, 'and ask them to call him in his room and tell him that Maya Richards is waiting for him in the lobby.'

'Wouldn't she go up to his room straight away?' he questioned.

'No, she wouldn't,' I explained. 'Five-star hotels like the Hyatt have certain procedures that they expect their guests to observe. Anyhow, even if our friend is surprised at the message, he's going to come down to see her.'

'But then, *Guruji*,' he said in a confused tone, 'when he doesn't find Maya Richards in the lobby but some strange girl beckoning him . . .' His voice tailed off.

'That's not the plan, Khargosh,' I said. 'After leaving this message with Reception, your girl will tell them that she's left her purse at home and she needs to pay off the taxi. She's waiting at the hotel front entrance, and, when Amit comes down and asks for her, they should tell him to go to the entrance.'

'That's perfect, *Guruji*,' said Khargosh in a satisfied manner.

'It doesn't solve all the problems of course, Khargosh. There will be a couple of those big security guards at the hotel's entrance. All five-stars employ these human giants to stand at the entrance.'

'Leave those details to me, *Guruji*,' said Khargosh, his voice supremely confident once more. 'We'll work out the rest. Once we've got this guy out into the main entrance, the rest will be easy. You've given us a good plan.' He paused. 'Do you have this woman Maya's mobile phone number?'

'I may have,' I said. 'Why do you ask?'

'I'll send you a text message just as we reach the hotel Reception. You'll then need to call Maya on her mobile and keep her phone busy for the next few minutes, just in case Amit decides to contact her.'

Khargosh was smart.

'I'll do that,' I said. 'I'm sure I have the number.'

In a few seconds I'd searched Ruhno's mobile phone address book and found Maya Richards's number.

We were making progress. The trap was about to close.

Shall I pour you another drink, Lord Patel? Another large one? Excellent.

21

Some of the creative minds here – yes, even lawyers at the Thirty Thousand Courts can be creative – have developed a hypothesis that the names of Scotch whisky are chosen because of their subversive character. I personally don't subscribe to this view but will repeat the claim anyhow for your entertainment. It's argued that Teachers and Vat 69, two very popular brands in India, are both ironic names. A teacher represents respectability and virtue of a kind that does not blend easily with whisky, even if it happens to be a fine Scotch. As for Vat 69, according to this theory the number 69 is actually the Pope's phone number in Vatican City, and you can't get more pious or virtuous than the Pope, can you – even if Jesus did turn water into wine. No, sir, you cannot imagine a drunken Pope. It would be sacrilege even to contemplate that. My neighbour Mr Bhushan, who is fairly religious himself, being a part-time priest, and completely abstemious as far as spirits are concerned, believes that the 'Vat' in Vat 69 merely refers to the vat or cask in which the whisky is matured, a perfectly reasonable explanation which I for one tend to find credible, whereas Mr Tomar, my other neighbour, who drinks regularly, had the epiphany during one of his drunken soirees that the number 69 might refer to a sexual position. I'm not convinced of that. Anyhow, the fact of the matter is that, whatever the merits of this hypothesis, the reason it has been advanced is possibly because this mischievous idea adds to the enjoyment of the drink.

Have you read Dostoevsky's *Crime and Punishment*, Lord Patel? It is the tale of a man who decides to kill someone who does not deserve to live, a grubby old money-lender. In some ways the book foresaw the Russian Revolution, where there would be a certain legitimacy to the killing of members of the bourgeoisie, the exploiting class, who carried on a perfectly legitimate business, you see, and there was no way to end this exploitation through the courts of justice. And I too, like the famous Raskolnikov, came to the realisation that Amit and Sunil did not deserve to live, they had done nothing for anyone, and there was no way of doing anything to them through the courts of law. For I know better than most people how the courts function.

But bringing Amit Patel and Sunil Gupta to justice was a job I could not accomplish alone. Khargosh was there to help, and, while he and his associates were enough to wreak retribution and vengeance on Sunil, in the case of your son Amit I needed additional collaborators. Fortunately for me, these were close at hand, and easy to co-opt. You see, Lord Patel, Ruhno came to my chambers a few times, on her way from the university to somewhere else. And such was her queenly grace, kindness and courtesy that Hetram and Saeed could not help but be charmed by her. Hetram in particular was in complete awe of Ruhno.

So on the day it had been decided that Khargosh and his associates would kidnap Amit – 'lift' him from the lobby of the Hyatt Regency – Saeed, Hetram and I were sitting in my chambers staring at my cellphone, awaiting news from Khargosh. He and I had gone over the plan once again, the night before, and discussed some of the final details.

'How are you going to bring him to my chambers?' I had asked Khargosh.

'What do you mean, *Guruji*?' he said.

'I mean you realise that you're not allowed to drive up to my chambers.'

I could hear him thinking.

'Don't worry, *Guruji*,' he said eventually. 'We'll find a way.' He paused, and then casually said 'You've been losing weight these past few months, *Guruji*. I'll bring you some potatoes.'

Already I had received a text message from Khargosh with the single word 'Reception'. As arranged, I immediately rang Maya Richards's mobile and hung up as soon as she picked up, then kept ringing on and off, keeping the phone busy for five minutes or more, until I thought Amit would have reached the hotel lobby. Just after six o'clock I stopped ringing.

As we awaited another call from Khargosh, a ping suddenly sounded on my cellphone – a new text message, which I hoped would mean only one thing. A cheer went up once I'd read the text and announced that Khargosh had made a successful snatch. At least that's what I assumed the cryptic message, 'Potatoes put in sack', was supposed to convey.

The minutes trickled past and there was no further news after the last ambiguous text. Had Khargosh and company been nabbed? Was he with the police? Where the hell was he? I called him several times but there was no response from his mobile.

Then an hour later I got a phone call.

'Where are you?' I shouted.

'Two minutes away,' he replied coolly. 'I didn't want to take your calls, because you never know these days. The police are very smart and they can listen in on anyone's conversation. Your phone may be tapped, even if you've changed your number. They are very smart, believe me, *Guruji*. But I've got your consignment with me and I will deliver it in . . . ten seconds.'

He was at the door to my chambers, with a tall, muscular young fellow with a chest as wide as the doorway, one of his gang members I guessed, and between the two of them they carried a huge sack in which I spotted – potatoes!

They threw the sack on the ground and I heard the sound of muffled squealing inside it. Khargosh took out a knife concealed inside one of his long leather boots and ripped the sack open. Out tumbled a hundred-odd potatoes and, lying on the floor in the middle of the mess, your son Amit, a brown cotton sheet wrapped tightly around him.

His hands and feet were tied and his mouth was gagged with a piece of cloth. I gave Saeed the nod, and he began to untie Amit's hands and feet. I should mention that it was after seven in the evening, but the light from my chambers and the streetlights close by were sufficient for us to see each other. This section of the lawyers' chambers – the 'civil side' that houses the offices of lawyers who mainly practise civil law – was deserted, unlike the chambers on the 'criminal side', where possibly a fair amount of comings and goings were still taking place.

Meanwhile, I quizzed Khargosh on how he had managed to 'lift' Amit in the presence of the giant doorman and the couple of security guards that one usually encounters outside the entrance to the lobby of any five-star hotel in Delhi.

'It was very easy, *Guruji*,' he said. 'You'd already provided us with the main plan to draw him out of the hotel building. When Anita – that's our smart, western-educated girl who helped us in this operation – told the young fool at Reception that she wanted Amit to come to the lobby entrance of the hotel, he agreed to convey that message. Himesh, one of our gang members' – he turned to the beefy young guy at his side – 'has a brother who drives a taxi, and we used his Maruti van for this operation . . .'

'After changing the number plates of his taxi, of course,' Himesh interjected.

'It was the sensible thing to do,' continued Khargosh. 'I was the taxi driver, and Himesh here was Anita's fellow passenger, who also didn't have money. Once Anita came out, I texted you to tell you it was time to call that woman . . . what's her name, yes, Maya . . . and keep her busy, and then Anita, Himesh and I did a small performance in front of the security guard in which I was demanding money and Anita and Himesh were saying, don't worry, our friend is coming with the money. I turned to the giant – you were right about his size, *Guruji* – and asked him if it would be better if we moved the taxi a bit closer to the car park, and if he could give a message to Amit Patel that we were waiting for him there. He looked at me and Himesh a bit suspiciously – don't forget, I was wearing a taxi driver's uniform – but Anita is so classy that he said, yes, that's a good idea, you need to move, otherwise you'll be blocking the traffic, I'll send Amit down below to the car park, it's only a short distance. Anita then gave him a description of Amit's appearance, and explained he would be at the lobby entrance in a few minutes. The giant said, don't worry, I'll recognise him and send him over.'

He chortled merrily and Himesh joined in the laughter.

'And that's how this idiot came into the car park a few minutes later. Practically walked into our arms. Anita shouted, "Amit!", and, a little confused, he walked towards the taxi, and in the meanwhile Himesh here came up behind him, poked a knife into his back, and told him to get in.'

'What about the potatoes?' I asked.

'That's what took us time, *Guruji*,' said Khargosh apologetically. 'We had to find a bedsheet and buy the potatoes and the guy was trying to cheat us. You know, they're only fifty rupees a kilo everywhere and he wanted seventy-five. Even when we were buying . . . how many, Billoo?' he turned to his companion. 'Fifteen kilos, wasn't it?'

'Well, you guys must be hungry now,' I said, 'with all that activity.'

'Hungry?' repeated Khargosh, not understanding.

Hetram, who was standing just next to us, smiled, went inside the chambers and came out with a small rectangular plastic tiffin box.

'It's all in five-hundred-rupee notes,' I said, giving the tiffin box to Khargosh, 'just as you wanted it. It's amazing the amount of money that can fit into a small lunchbox.'

Khargosh and Himesh chuckled.

'We'll be getting along then, *Guruji*,' said Khargosh. 'I'll drop in next week. I have a court hearing coming up.'

* * *

Your hand is raised, Lord Patel, like a pupil seeking permission to leave the classroom. Do you wish to go to the toilet? No problem, there is one close by. We are rather better equipped to deal with such natural emergencies than Nathu's. It's just round the corner. Let me step outside and show you. Careful, the platform to the chambers is a bit higher than usual. Can you see that place where the hanging bulb without the shade is burning? That's the place. It's always kept open just in case a lawyer wants to work late, and the security men who are posted at the main entrance and who guard our offices through the night use it themselves. In the meanwhile, I will make another drink for both of us. The last one, you say. Very well. Let it be the last one.

22

Welcome back, Lord Patel. Your drink is ready, and it will be the last one for both of us, since the half-bottle is finished. Well done, I might say, to both of us.

And so, as I was telling you, after Khargosh and his muscular friend had delivered the 'consignment' – another term of the trade that he used – and collected the payment, they left. Meanwhile, Saeed had pushed Amit into my chambers and made him sit on one of the hard-backed chairs, which was suited to an interrogation. He and Hetram took the more comfortable chairs.

Then Saeed ungagged your son. He still had a bit of spirit left in him, and I could see that he was about to start shouting and screaming, but the first cry had barely left his mouth when Saeed hit him hard across the face. Three times. The shock of it stopped him in his tracks. He was quiet after that, and shot a pleading glance at me.

'Please let me go,' he begged. 'I'm sorry for what happened.'

He fell silent again, aware that he had touched a raw nerve. Now was the time to get him to talk.

'We spoke to your friend Sunil Gupta,' I lied, 'before punching a few holes inside him with a sharp knife and throwing him overboard into the Yamuna. And he told us something about what you had planned that evening at Jhilmil Lake.'

Amit was watching me the way a bird might look at a snake that was about to swallow it. He was fearful, but had the intelligence to try to exaggerate his fear just a little, in the hope that it would get him some pity. Khargosh and his friends had already roughed him up before putting him into the sack of potatoes, so I'm sure he didn't find it difficult. Besides, Saeed's glowering face was enough to inspire fear in anyone.

'He told us . . .' I carried on with the story, the telling becoming more difficult as I progressed. 'He told us that you had planned it between yourselves that after you had made love to Ruhno you would give him a missed call – ring his mobile and then hang up – and he would leave the cafeteria for the cottage, and take the keys from you, while you yourself were driving back to the White House. You told Ruhno you were just going to the cafeteria to ask them to send some coffee, didn't you?' I paused. 'You knew she liked coffee. Sunil told us that this had been your idea.'

Amit's expression fell when he heard all this, as if he now knew that there was no hope for him. I could see clearly from the look on his face that he didn't disbelieve a word of what I said. And that was because it was so accurate.

His expression confirmed the truth of what I'd said, and this realisation hit me like a physical blow. I was so overcome that I couldn't speak any more.

Meanwhile Saeed started to work on him. He hadn't even begun the 'treatment', Lord Patel, when your son quite literally peed in his pants and confessed everything. Saeed had only taken out a six-inch serrated knife made in Banaras, when – surprise, surprise! – the great Lord Patel's worthless son began to sob and beg for forgiveness.

Yes, he admitted, it was true, but it had not been his idea at all. Trying to make up lost ground, he insisted that it had been Sunil Gupta's plan from the start. It was Sunil who had let some of his girlfriends (possibly from the wife-swapping club in his previous assignment) sleep with Amit, and, for him, sleeping with Ruhno was payback. Sunil had also argued that the best way to 'teach Ruhno her place' was for her to have sex, even forced sex, with him, Sunil Gupta. This would effectively kill all her romantic ideas of a wedding with Amit. Sunil argued that she wouldn't mind because she had already lost her virginity to Amit. Even after the episode, his guess was that she would continue to work for Patel Holdings and Properties, on their terms. And if she did not, so be it. Consultants with her kind of over-theoretical knowledge were a penny a dozen.

All this was recounted by Amit, not in the way I'm narrating it to you, but in sobbing tones of regret, which I have excised, because the expression of regret was born of his situation that day, the hope that it would save his life, and it wasn't something that he really felt or believed. And even if he did, what did I care?

For this particular occasion, a week earlier I had bought one of those cute new-fangled gadgets the size of a small torch containing instead a small-sized tape with a capacity of three hours' recording. While Amit was blabbing on about the whole sordid saga, the tape was running.

For me, at that point, Lord Patel, it really didn't matter who had been the originator of the plan for Sunil to have forced sex with Ruhno. More likely, it was Sunil, I grant you that. Yet Amit had been the one with whom Ruhno had thought she was having a meaningful relationship; the person on whose behalf she had fought with me, her brother; the person with whom she had held romantic notions of marriage and children; and the person she had trusted and had put misplaced faith in. Possibly even in her dying moments she had not fully understood or believed the nature of the conspiracy – such a breach of faith and trust would have been beyond the comprehension of her innocent mind, for surely otherwise she would have revealed Amit's name as well. But she hadn't. She had only spoken of Sunil Gupta's rape. And she had mentioned the open door and the coffee that Amit had gone to fetch, which at the time I had mistaken for a request she was making to me for coffee.

I thought back to my visit to Jhilmil Lake a few months earlier. The *pahadi* waiter had told me that Sunil had taken a table on the other side of the cafeteria, with a clear view of Cottage 16. I had chosen to sit in the section that had a lakeside view. Despite being keen to meet the attendant of the cottage, I had wanted to look at the lake, in the hope that it would make me think more clearly.

And then Sunil hadn't even finished the double omelette that he had ordered, and had suddenly rushed off. Why? Amit gave him a missed call from the room, after having had sex with Ruhno. He then told Ruhno that he was going to the cafeteria to order some coffee. Once Sunil received the missed call, his eyes were glued to the cottage, and as soon as he saw Amit exit, he left everything and hurried to the cottage, where Amit gave him the keys to open the door which would have shut automatically behind him.

And so he entered, and Ruhno, poor girl, was still in a state of undress. She saw him and screamed, and at that moment the young lad came over with the keys that Sunil had left behind inside the cafeteria. He heard the screams, but was stopped from going any further by Ranvir Singh, who took the keys from him and told him to get lost. This was a stunt that Sunil had probably pulled in the past as well, possibly from Cottage 16 itself, where Ranvir Singh acted as his scout and prevented any third person from entering.

Do I need to say anything more, Lord Patel?

We gave him some whisky to help loosen his tongue. Hetram was the bartender that day, mixing the drinks for me, Saeed and Amit, despite being a teetotaller himself, a vow he had taken some years earlier on a visit to the shrine of Mata Vaishno Devi. I took my whisky with soda, Saeed took his with water, and, as far as your son Amit was concerned, Hetram took care to surreptitiously pour in a few spoons of an Ayurvedic mixture that he had spent the previous three days preparing. It had to be effective, you see, and yet not spoil the taste of the whisky. Wouldn't want to waste good Scotch whisky, Lord Patel, even if it was your worthless son who happened to be drinking it. Ah yes, I should mention that Hetram told me that one of the ingredients of the mixture he had dreamed up was very useful in killing cockroaches and rats. And I told him, well, that will be suitable for Amit Patel then, won't it?

After the fourth or fifth glass, the poison began to have a visible effect on Amit. The colour of his skin began to change, and his voice, which had initially started to slur, now became a squeak. At this point, Hetram, poor fellow, felt a bit squeamish and expressed his wish to go home. I fully understood his feelings and didn't press him to stay. If it hadn't been my own sister who had lost her life, my reaction would probably have been very similar to his. As things stood, however, Ruhno's sobbing face kept flashing before my eyes, and so my resolve was firm, even as your son continued to drink his whisky. So Hetram left the chamber apologetically, pointing out quite rightly that he needed to rush, else he would miss the last train to Baghpat.

You want to know if we actually killed your son? No torture, Lord Patel. He died drinking Scotch whisky. The same brand that you have just enjoyed. Vat 69. Six very strong measures. Strong enough to disguise the taste of an Ayurvedic preparation used to kill rats. It was appropriate, *comme il faut*, don't you think? But you are his father, so you wouldn't think so. Hetram fixed his drinks, and we drank alongside, although we had ours without any additions – neat, as they say. Hetram took his with some orange juice. He doesn't usually drink, you see, but that day it was an occasion to celebrate, in a way.

In the end everything worked out. I received a big pile of cash from Kumar Jain (and so did Bihari) for getting his property vacated, and this was usefully spent on the initial construction work on the basement, then covering it up, paying off Khargosh and his gang, giving Saeed enough capital for him to start up as a building contractor once again, and giving Hetram enough money to go on another *yatra* to Mata Vaishno Devi.

Mr Bhushan and Mr Tomar, my neighbours at the court, knew I didn't have much business, so they were intrigued when they saw that I had begun work on the construction of a basement to my chambers. Was I planning it for business, they wanted to know.

'Strictly pleasure,' I'd responded.

Tomar was pleased. He had whisky parties regularly in his chambers, which I sometimes attended, so as not to be rude, you understand. 'We'll have a good time in your chambers!' he said with a grin. 'Drinks at mine, and then for extras we come to yours. You won't deny us, will you?'

Bhushan uttered a word of caution. 'There are some underground water pipes around this place. Be careful you don't burst one of those.'

Tomar leered at me in a friendly fashion. 'It will be very useful to have that extra space,' he said. 'If you wanted to have a quick nap after lunch, you could. And then later in the evening you could "de-stress" with one of the finer ladies from the Western Bloc before going home.'

Bhushan smirked. As a part-time priest in a Kali Devi temple, he was himself a vegetarian and teetotaller – never, as I occasionally did, joining Tomar's evening parties (unless it was to listen to gossip) – but he liked talking about women. 'There is a very fine woman you should call over,' he said in a confiding tone. 'Saw her with Mr Rias Ahmed a week ago at his chambers on the criminal side. Absolutely perfect breasts. Firm and upright like two Himalayan peaks.'

Tomar chortled at his friend's description.

It was his words that give me my plan. I had needed an excuse for stopping the construction of the basement, for refilling it with mud and sand, and Bhushan had just supplied me with the reason I could give everyone.

Yes, Lord Patel, it was exactly as I had suspected. And after his confession – the stupid boy – his life, of course, could not be spared. I had admitted to myself that there was a small possibility that I was wrong, that I had misunderstood the meaning of Ruhno's last words, but alas for Amit, and more alas for me, I had been exactly right. So we killed him. There was no choice.

When you came here this morning you were curious about why my chambers was built at an elevation. Well spotted. And I told you that I didn't want the water getting inside the chambers during the monsoons. That wasn't really the reason. By all accounts, as far as my lawyer colleagues were concerned, I was constructing a basement for my chambers. I sat at an elevation, and the work continued downstairs. The reality, of course, was something very different. You see, Lord Patel, I began digging your son's grave as soon as I realised what had happened on the day my sister had visited Jhilmil Lake.

You also spotted a few nails on the wall behind me, and I explained that there had been a set of bookshelves but that the walls weren't strong enough to take the weight of the shelves as well as the books. I'm not sure how strong these walls are – possibly the materials used may not have been very strong – but the purpose of those shelves was something different. It was Saeed who gave me the idea.

'Let's give him a proper burial, if you agree,' he had said. 'I'll get one of the carpenters I know to make a bookcase for you which can double up as a coffin. We can just hang the shelves on the wall by a few nails – don't put any books on them, and tell anyone who asks that the carpenter has gone off to attend a wedding for a few days. We'll make it such that a human being can fit in sideways – how big is this fellow?'

I told him that he was of slight build, a fourteen-inch collar size.

'That's okay then,' he said. 'We'll get two bookshelves and remove the central plank – and use it to cover the box. Won't take two minutes. I've worked on these kinds of designs before. Just leave this to me.'

All right, I had said, I'll leave it to you.

So not only did I not torture your son – which under the circumstances you will grant that I was fully entitled to do – but I also gave him a decent burial. After the fifth drink, his head suddenly slumped on the table, and when we felt for his pulse we couldn't find it. Saeed took out some tools, removed the makeshift bookcase hanging on the wall, and within a few minutes had assembled it into a very elegant-looking coffin into which we then lowered your son's body. Not immediately. I normally have a couple of coat brushes inside my office cupboard – there is so much dust flying around these parts, and you don't want to enter the courtroom looking untidy and sloppy – so we brushed his coat and trousers, so that the soil from the potatoes was cleared up. I had recorded his confession on a CD, by the way, and I made a copy of it for my own records. As we placed his body into the coffin, I put the original CD on which his confession was recorded into his coat pocket.

Saeed and I then lifted the coffin with the body inside and went down the stairs into the basement. Saeed had prepared a rectangular hole in the ground based on the coffin's measurements in the time Hetram and I had been upstairs trying to reach Khargosh on the phone. The coffin neatly fitted into that hole, and then we got busy laying out bricks all over the floor. I have to say that I had no energy remaining for this kind of work, so I left Saeed all alone downstairs to work with the bricks and the cement.

During the course of the afternoon and the evening, Saeed got Hetram to help him do some preliminary bricklaying in anticipation that Khargosh's mission would be successful. The labourers he had employed for the construction of the half-completed basement could no longer be used for the more sensitive job of filling up the basement again. This was a job he had to do himself, either alone or with someone trusted like Hetram. And now the poor fellow was alone in this task.

I came up and began to drink what remained of the bottle of Vat 69 through the rest of the night. It was early morning by the time that Saeed had managed to place enough bricks, packed tightly with cement, over the coffin.

He then went to his stall and opened it up. The lads who work for him had not yet arrived, so he prepared the tea himself and came to my chambers with a cup for both of us, together with the *fains* that you had the opportunity to sample this morning – but did not like very much, I think.

After we had eaten this simple breakfast, I took out the money I had promised him, so that he could set himself up in the construction trade once again, and gave it to him. So you will want to know, no doubt, why is he still around. Well, you see, he has decided to leave Delhi and set up business in some other city. The reason he hasn't gone till now is because he is trying to find a good price for his stall. Yes, Lord Patel, even the ramshackle shacks that you have seen outside have some property value, rather higher than one might estimate at first glance, a hundred thousand rupees at the very minimum, though you wouldn't think it to look at them.

He has finally found a buyer – one of the rival tea stall owners, who wishes to run his place as a shop selling lawyers' ties and gowns. He came to say goodbye to me two days ago. I mentioned that I had invited you over, and he said he wished to have a look at you. The man whose son he helped to kill and bury. The great Lord Patel. Even Saeed has heard of you. And that is the reason, dear sir, that you caught him staring at you this morning in that funny fashion.

You might wonder why I didn't keep a basement. After all, I could have buried your son in the ground and continued to have a basement. The reason for this is that Bhushan was actually right when he said there was possibly a water pipe running through the ground beneath my chamber. It was just two feet below where we had already dug down to, so with the space needed to give your son a decent burial it wouldn't really have been possible to have a decent-sized basement. Still, I could have had a very low-ceilinged basement, but on reflection I decided I wanted to put a few extra feet of space between your son's body and my office. Afraid of ghosts? Not really. Just a sense of propriety and delicacy, I think.

Tomar and Bhushan came over a couple of days later to see the progress. I told them that the basement proposal had been abandoned. I explained that the water pipe ran too close, at which Bhushan said, 'I told you so.' Tomar then noticed that my pinewood bookshelves were missing.

'I've decided to use them for the office I keep at my residence,' I had lied. 'I don't want to scare off the poorer clients who come here by having such fancy furniture.'

'That's right,' Tomar had chuckled. 'I'm actually relieved to see them gone. I was feeling under some pressure to carry out some renovation in my own office, but now I'm relaxed.' We had all laughed.

Didn't you send your son to work in India to ground him? To give him a sense of his own culture? To let him know where his roots lay? You nod your head. It was all these things, wasn't it?

Plus the fact that you had heard he was getting up to no good in London, New York and other western capitals where you have your offices. Your company recently took over one of the biggest copper companies in West Africa. Surely you would have asked him to manage it, if you hadn't worried that he would end up wasting his time with women and drugs.

Who says that there is no justice in the world? Even the Thirty Thousand Courts can provide justice. The fact that your son's bones are rotting beneath the floor of my chambers is surely proof enough of the capacity of these courts to provide justice.

I told you that I would take you to your son, Lord Patel, and I have fulfilled my promise. You are at the present moment quite literally standing over your son's grave, or shall I say sitting over his grave, if you want me to be precise. I have brought you to him, and this is as close as you will get, for somehow I don't think you will want his body to be exhumed.

Ah, I can hear the sound of police sirens. Of course you parked your car near the main entrance to the courts and walked all the way here, for the *chowkidaar* would not let you drive across to the lawyers' chambers, but there cannot be any such restrictions imposed on the police. The last time I heard these sirens from my office was when they came to get Haji Sultan, the notorious diamond smuggler, who was hiding in his lawyer's basement. Perhaps you sent someone a text message from your mobile when you went for a pee just now. That's what you must have done. You are a clever fellow indeed.

Oh, it looks like you *are* nodding off, Mr Patel. I think by the time the police arrive you won't be in a position to say very much. You'll be rushed off to one of our five star hospitals, meant for the rich and superrich, people like yourself, where they will pump your stomach free of toxins. You will remain there for at least a day, perhaps two, but then you'll be fine. In your inner coat pocket you will find the tape of your son's confessions, which I placed there as you went off to the toilet. There are more where that copy came from. Do make sure it doesn't get into the wrong hands. It is not a pretty tale that your son Amit tells about himself and how he, together with Sunil planned the rape of my sister.

You might want me to be prosecuted but at what cost, Mr Patel? At what cost? These days the courts are sympathetic to rape victims, and any trial against me is likely to drag on for years and might even end up in an acquittal. When a man, in this case your son, confesses to a loving brother that he was the perpetrator of a rape on his sister, does that not constitute grave and sudden provocation? The reputation of your son will however be permanently tarnished as will your family name. There will be endless reports and analysis in the media about the tapes, and someone is bound to upload them on to YouTube for the world to listen to.

I know this has been a trauma for you, but you have only received a dose of Hetram's Ayurvedic preparations so that are temporarily immobilised and you take no hasty action, and this case of 'food poisoning,' as it were, will give you time to think long and hard about the matter. By the time you recover in hospital and have had time to ponder over the issue, I have a feeling that you will come round to my point of view that we should let the dead rest in peace....